Real Stories of Infamous Heists

Shah Rukh

Published by Shah Rukh, 2024.

REAL STORIES OF INFAMOUS HEISTS

First edition. May 12, 2024.

Copyright © 2024 Shah Rukh.

ISBN: 979-8224620661

Written by Shah Rukh.

Table of Contents

Prologue

In the dead of night, while the world sleeps, shadows move stealthily, orchestrating plans that have taken months—sometimes years—to perfect. The thrill of the heist is as old as time itself, a compelling dance between the hunter and the hunted, the thief and the law. From daring escapades in the Wild West to intricate cyber heists in the digital age, these stories of notorious robberies are bound together by a common thread: the audacity of those who dared to defy the odds and seize their moment in history.

This book takes you on a journey through the most infamous heists the world has ever known—each one a gripping tale of cunning and courage, of careful planning and desperate risk. Some of these stories have become legendary, capturing the public's imagination and inspiring countless books, movies, and folklore. Others remain shrouded in mystery, their secrets locked away with those who pulled them off.

What drives a person to attempt such a bold crime? Is it greed, desperation, or the thrill of outsmarting the system? As we dive into these narratives, we'll explore not just the facts and figures but the motivations behind the crimes. We'll meet a cast of characters as varied and colorful as any in fiction—masterminds and mavericks, double-crossers and desperate souls, each with their own unique story to tell.

Prepare to be amazed by the ingenuity and nerve of those who planned the unthinkable and executed the impossible. From the meticulous planning stages to the nail-biting moments of execution, from unexpected twists to stunning turns of fate, these stories will keep you on the edge of your seat. You'll encounter heists that were meticulously planned and brilliantly executed, as well as those that went disastrously wrong. Some ended in spectacular failure, others in windfalls beyond imagination, and a few in eternal mystery.

As you turn the pages, remember: every story you read here is not a tale spun from imagination, but a real-life account of the boldest crimes ever committed. Welcome to the world of infamous heists, where fact is stranger—and often far more thrilling—than fiction.

Let the adventure begin.

Chapter 1: The Disappearing D.B. Cooper

On the evening of November 24, 1971, a man using the alias "Dan Cooper" (later mistakenly referred to as D.B. Cooper) boarded Northwest Orient Airlines Flight 305 in Portland, Oregon, bound for Seattle, Washington. What transpired over the next few hours would etch his name into American folklore and history, as Cooper executed one of the most audacious and mysterious crimes in aviation history. The hijacking of Flight 305 is not just a tale of criminal daring; it is a story of intrigue, ingenuity, and an enduring enigma that has baffled law enforcement and captivated the public for over five decades.

The Skyjacking: A Bold Move

Dressed in a business suit, white shirt, black tie, and sunglasses, Cooper appeared to be an unremarkable, middle-aged man. He paid for his ticket in cash and boarded the plane without arousing any suspicion. Once airborne, Cooper handed a note to flight attendant Florence Schaffner, who initially assumed it was another lonely businessman offering his phone number. However, the note contained a far more sinister message: Cooper claimed to have a bomb in his briefcase and demanded $200,000 in unmarked bills, four parachutes, and a fuel truck standing by in Seattle to refuel the plane.

When Schaffner, still uncertain if the threat was real, asked to see the bomb, Cooper obligingly opened his briefcase to reveal a tangle of wires, red sticks, and a battery. The threat was clear, and the crew had no choice but to comply. Captain William Scott contacted Seattle-Tacoma Airport and relayed Cooper's demands. The authorities quickly gathered the ransom money and parachutes, preparing for the plane's arrival.

The Exchange: A Chilling Calmness

Despite the tense situation, Cooper remained calm and polite, even offering to pay for his drinks. The plane circled Puget Sound for nearly two hours to allow Seattle authorities to prepare his ransom and parachutes. Once the plane landed in Seattle, Cooper allowed all 36 passengers to disembark in exchange for the ransom and parachutes, demonstrating a curious blend of cold calculation and courtesy. The only people he kept on board were the pilot, the co-pilot, a flight attendant, and the flight engineer.

After the exchange, Cooper instructed the pilot to set a course for Mexico City, flying at an altitude of 10,000 feet and at a speed of no more than 200 knots, with the landing gear down and the cabin unpressurized. He also demanded that the rear exit door remain open during the flight. This request was unusual and dangerous, but it soon became clear why Cooper wanted it that way.

The Jump: Into the Unknown

Around 8:00 p.m., approximately 40 minutes after takeoff from Seattle, somewhere over the dense forests of southwestern Washington, Cooper opened the rear stairway of the Boeing 727 and jumped into the night, clutching the ransom money and wearing one of the parachutes. The crew, who had remained in the cockpit, did not see him jump, but they felt the plane's tail section pitch upwards as the rear stairway was lowered.

Cooper's jump was fraught with risks. The weather was stormy, with heavy rain and strong winds, and the terrain below was rugged and forested. The conditions were so bad that even experienced skydivers would have hesitated to jump. Moreover, Cooper had no way of knowing his exact location when he leaped, making his survival seem even more improbable.

The Investigation: An Unsolvable Puzzle

The moment Cooper disappeared into the night; he became a legend. The FBI launched one of the most extensive manhunts in U.S. history, known as NORJAK (Northwest Hijacking). Hundreds of agents combed the dense forests of the Pacific Northwest, searching for any sign of Cooper or the money. Military aircraft were scrambled to follow the hijacked plane, but the inclement weather and dense forest cover made it impossible to track him visually.

Despite the vast resources devoted to the search, no trace of Cooper was found. The FBI interviewed hundreds of suspects, pursued countless leads, and even conducted several re-enactments of the jump, but the trail went cold. The only physical evidence recovered was a small number of bills, with serial numbers matching the ransom money, found in 1980 on the banks of the Columbia River near Vancouver, Washington. This discovery only deepened the mystery, as it raised more questions than it answered. How had the money ended up there? Had Cooper survived the jump, or had he perished in the wilderness, leaving the money to wash downstream?

Theories and Suspects: A Mystery That Endures

Over the years, numerous theories have been proposed regarding Cooper's fate. Some believe he died in the jump, overwhelmed by the harsh conditions and rugged terrain. Others think he survived and lived out the rest of his life in anonymity. The case has generated a wide array of suspects, some more plausible than others.

One of the earliest suspects was a man named Richard Floyd McCoy, who was arrested for a similar hijacking just five months after Cooper's. McCoy's physical description and modus operandi bore striking similarities to Cooper's, leading some to believe he was the man behind both hijackings. However, the FBI ultimately ruled him out, citing differences in age and appearance, as well as the lack of direct evidence linking him to the Cooper case.

Another suspect was Duane Weber, who allegedly confessed to being Cooper on his deathbed in 1995. His widow, Jo Weber, claimed that Duane had shown knowledge of details related to the case that were not publicly known. However, the FBI was unable to conclusively link Weber to the crime, and his fingerprints did not match any found on the plane.

Other suspects include Vietnam veteran Kenneth Christiansen, who had flight experience and a possible motive, and Robert Rackstraw, a former Army pilot with a history of deception and legal troubles. While these individuals have compelling connections to the case, none of them have been definitively proven to be D.B. Cooper.

The Cultural Impact: A Legend That Lives On

D.B. Cooper has become a cultural icon, symbolizing the ultimate outlaw who outwitted the authorities and vanished without a trace. His story has inspired countless books, documentaries, movies, and even songs. The enduring fascination with Cooper stems not only from the audacity of his crime but also from the mystery that surrounds it. Unlike other famous criminals, whose stories eventually end in capture or death, Cooper's tale remains open-ended, inviting endless speculation and debate.

The FBI officially closed the case in 2016, citing a lack of new evidence, but interest in the case remains high. Amateur sleuths, known as "Cooperites," continue to pore over old files, search the forests of the Pacific Northwest, and debate theories in online forums. The case has also inspired annual D.B. Cooper-themed events, including skydiving exhibitions and look-alike contests.

Conclusion: The Unsolved Enigma

The story of D.B. Cooper is a unique chapter in American criminal history, distinguished by its blend of daring, mystery, and intrigue. Despite decades of investigation and countless theories, the true identity and fate of D.B. Cooper remain unknown. His successful hijacking and subsequent disappearance are not only a testament to his planning and audacity but also a reminder of the limits of modern law enforcement.

The case continues to captivate the public imagination, serving as a reminder that some mysteries may never be fully resolved. D.B. Cooper, whoever he was, has secured a place in history as one of the most enigmatic and elusive figures in the annals of crime. His story is a complex tapestry woven from equal parts fact, speculation, and myth—a story that will likely continue to intrigue and mystify for generations to come.

Chapter 2: The Alaskan Gold Rush Heist

The Alaskan Gold Rush, which took place in the late 19th and early 20th centuries, was a period of intense excitement, hardship, and fortune-seeking that drew thousands of prospectors to the frozen wilderness of the Yukon and Alaska. It was an era characterized by wild ambition, immense challenges, and the dream of striking it rich. Yet, amidst the stories of fortune and adventure, there lies a tale of one of the most daring and mysterious heists in the annals of American history—The Alaskan Gold Rush Heist. This audacious crime, set against the backdrop of the rugged Alaskan frontier, is a story of greed, betrayal, and the ultimate disappearance of a fortune in gold that has never been recovered.

The Background: A Land of Opportunity and Danger

In the late 1800s, the discovery of gold in the Klondike region of Canada's Yukon Territory set off one of the last great gold rushes in North American history. Thousands of men and women, known as "stampeders," flocked to the region, enduring brutal conditions, treacherous terrain, and extreme weather in the hope of striking it rich. The journey to the gold fields was perilous, with many facing starvation, disease, and even death along the way.

As word spread of rich gold deposits in the Klondike, the stampede extended into Alaska, where prospectors hoped to find new, untapped veins of the precious metal. The small towns and ports along the coast, such as Skagway and Nome, quickly transformed into bustling centers of activity, filled with miners, traders, and opportunists of all kinds. These towns became the launching points for expeditions into the interior, where gold fever gripped the hearts of those who ventured into the untamed wilderness.

But with the influx of gold and the lawlessness of the frontier came the inevitable rise in crime. Robberies, scams, and violence were common in these rough-and-tumble communities, where the lure of easy riches could bring out the worst in people. It was in this volatile environment that the Alaskan Gold Rush Heist took place, a crime so audacious that it has become one of the great legends of the Gold Rush era.

The Heist: A Bold Plan Takes Shape

The Alaskan Gold Rush Heist was not a spur-of-the-moment crime, but rather the result of careful planning and a deep understanding of the region's dynamics. The gold was typically transported from the interior mining camps to coastal towns like Nome or Skagway, where it would be loaded onto steamships bound for the lower United States. These shipments were heavily guarded, as they represented the life savings and dreams of countless prospectors.

However, even with tight security, there were vulnerabilities. The remote and rugged terrain of Alaska made it difficult to maintain a continuous line of defense, and the sheer volume of gold being moved during the height of the rush created opportunities for those daring enough to take the risk.

The masterminds behind the Alaskan Gold Rush Heist were a group of seasoned outlaws who had spent years in the region, learning the lay of the land and understanding the movement of gold shipments. They knew that striking a shipment at the right time and place could yield a fortune beyond their wildest dreams. Their plan was simple but effective: ambush a shipment of gold in transit, overpower the guards, and disappear into the wilderness with the loot.

The Execution: A Crime in the Dead of Night

The chosen target was a particularly large shipment of gold, estimated to be worth over a million dollars at the time—a staggering sum in the late 19th century. The shipment was scheduled to be transported from the mining camps near the town of Nome to the coastal port, where it would be loaded onto a steamship headed for Seattle. The outlaws knew the exact route the shipment would take and the timing of the transport, giving them the perfect opportunity to strike.

On a cold, moonless night, the gang set their plan into motion. They positioned themselves along a remote stretch of the trail, far from any settlements or law enforcement. As the stagecoach carrying the gold made its way through the wilderness, the outlaws launched their ambush. The guards, though experienced, were caught off guard by the sudden attack. Outnumbered and outgunned, they were quickly subdued by the bandits.

With the guards neutralized, the outlaws made quick work of securing the gold. They loaded the heavy sacks of gold dust and nuggets onto their horses and disappeared into the night, leaving the stunned guards tied up and helpless in the wilderness. The entire heist took only a matter of minutes, yet it would become one of the most infamous crimes of the Gold Rush era.

The Aftermath: A Massive Manhunt

News of the heist spread quickly, sending shockwaves through the mining community and beyond. The loss of such a large shipment of gold was devastating to the miners who had worked so hard to extract it from the earth, and it represented a significant blow to the economy of the region. Law enforcement, already stretched thin in the remote Alaskan frontier, launched a massive manhunt to track down the perpetrators and recover the stolen gold.

Posse after posse was sent into the wilderness, following every lead and searching for any sign of the outlaws. But the rugged terrain and harsh weather worked in favor of the bandits, who had carefully planned their escape route through some of the most inhospitable terrain in the region. Weeks turned into months, and despite the best efforts of the authorities, no trace of the outlaws or the gold was found.

The heist quickly became the stuff of legend, with rumors and speculation running wild. Some believed the outlaws had perished in the wilderness, unable to survive the harsh conditions with their heavy load of gold. Others speculated that they had managed to escape to the lower United States or even to a foreign country, where they could live out their days in luxury. Still, others thought that the gold had been hidden somewhere in the vast Alaskan wilderness, waiting to be discovered by some lucky prospector.

Theories and Speculation: Where Did the Gold Go?

As time passed, the mystery of the Alaskan Gold Rush Heist only deepened. Numerous theories emerged about the fate of the gold and the outlaws who had stolen it. Some claimed that the bandits had buried the gold in a secret location, intending to return for it later, but were unable to do so due to unforeseen circumstances. This theory gained traction when, years later, a few small caches of gold were discovered in remote areas, far from any known mining sites. However, these finds were never definitively linked to the heist, and the bulk of the stolen gold remained missing.

Another popular theory was that the outlaws had managed to smuggle the gold out of Alaska and had melted it down to obscure its origins. This would have made it difficult for authorities to trace the gold, allowing the thieves to sell it off in small amounts over time. Supporters of this theory pointed to the fact that gold was a relatively easy commodity to move and convert into cash, especially in the bustling markets of the West Coast during the Gold Rush era.

There were also those who believed that the outlaws had met a tragic end, either at the hands of nature or through internal betrayal. The harsh conditions of the Alaskan wilderness were unforgiving, and it was not uncommon for people to disappear without a trace in the remote regions. If the bandits had been caught in a blizzard, fallen into a crevasse, or suffered some other misfortune, their bodies—and the gold—could have easily been lost forever.

The Legacy: A Tale of Greed and Mystery

The Alaskan Gold Rush Heist remains one of the great unsolved mysteries of the American frontier. Despite the passage of more than a century, the fate of the stolen gold and the identity of the outlaws who pulled off the daring heist are still unknown. The story has become a part of Alaskan folklore, passed down through generations and embellished over time.

The heist also serves as a reminder of the lawlessness and danger that characterized the Gold Rush era. While the promise of untold wealth drew thousands of people to the region, it also attracted those who were willing to take extreme risks to achieve their own fortunes, even at the expense of others. The outlaws behind the Alaskan Gold Rush Heist were emblematic of the darker side of the Gold Rush, where the line between right and wrong was often blurred in the pursuit of riches.

In modern times, the story of the heist has inspired countless treasure hunters, amateur sleuths, and adventurers to search for the lost gold. Some have scoured the Alaskan wilderness, hoping to find clues or hidden caches that might solve the mystery. Others have delved into historical records, trying to piece together the identities of the outlaws and their possible fates. Yet, despite these efforts, the mystery endures, as elusive and tantalizing as the gold itself.

Conclusion: A Mystery for the Ages

The Alaskan Gold Rush Heist is a story of ambition, greed, and the enduring allure of lost treasure. It captures the imagination with its combination of historical intrigue, adventure, and the possibility that the stolen fortune might still be out there, waiting to be discovered. The heist is a testament to the lengths that some were willing to go during the Gold Rush era, and it stands as one of the most enigmatic and captivating tales from that period in American history.

Whether the gold was lost to the elements, hidden away by the outlaws, or smuggled out of Alaska and dispersed over time, the true fate of the stolen treasure remains a mystery. The story of the Alaskan Gold Rush Heist continues to intrigue and inspire, a reminder that some of the greatest stories from the past are those that have yet to be fully told. As long as the gold remains missing, the legend of the heist will endure, a tantalizing puzzle for future generations to ponder and explore.

Chapter 3: The Great Train Robbery of the Old West

The expansion of the American West in the 19th century was fueled by the construction of railroads that connected the vast, untamed territories to the more developed regions of the eastern United States. These iron arteries became the lifelines of commerce, transporting goods, cattle, and people across the sprawling landscape. However, the very success of the railroads also made them targets for one of the most infamous criminal activities of the Old West: train robbery. Among the many such crimes, none are as legendary as "The Great Train Robbery of the Old West," a daring and meticulously planned heist that captured the imagination of the nation and became a symbol of the lawless and adventurous spirit of the frontier.

The Setting: A Land of Opportunity and Lawlessness

The mid-to-late 1800s was a period of rapid growth and development in the United States, especially in the western territories. The discovery of gold and other valuable resources led to a rush of settlers and fortune-seekers heading west, creating boomtowns almost overnight. The construction of the transcontinental railroad, completed in 1869, further accelerated this movement, making travel and transportation of goods faster and more efficient.

However, with opportunity came risk. The vast distances and rugged terrain made law enforcement difficult, and the rapid influx of settlers often outpaced the establishment of formal legal systems. The result was a volatile environment where outlaws could operate with relative impunity, taking advantage of the sparse and often under-resourced law enforcement.

Train robberies became a particularly lucrative crime during this period. Trains often carried large sums of money, gold, and other valuable cargo, making them tempting targets for outlaws. Moreover, the isolated stretches of track that cut through desolate landscapes provided ample opportunity for ambushes, where robbers could strike swiftly and then disappear into the wilderness before lawmen could respond.

The Outlaws: The Rise of Notorious Bandits

The Great Train Robbery of the Old West was carried out by a group of seasoned outlaws who had honed their skills through years of criminal activity. Among the most notorious were members of the James-Younger Gang, led by the infamous Jesse James and his brother Frank. The James brothers, along with their cohorts, were veterans of the Civil War, where they had fought as Confederate guerrillas. The war had hardened them, and they brought their experience in guerrilla tactics to their criminal enterprises.

Jesse James, in particular, had become something of a folk hero, admired by some as a modern-day Robin Hood who robbed from the rich and fought against the perceived injustices of the Union victors. This image, however, was more myth than reality. In truth, the James-Younger Gang was a ruthless and efficient criminal organization, responsible for numerous bank and train robberies, as well as murders.

Another key player in the Great Train Robbery was the Reno Gang, a group of brothers and their associates who are often credited with carrying out the first peacetime train robbery in the United States. The Reno brothers—Frank, John, Simeon, and William—were notorious criminals from Indiana who turned to train robbery as a way to escape the law and make quick money. Their activities would set the stage for many more train heists to come, including the one that would become known as the Great Train Robbery of the Old West.

The Heist: Planning and Execution

The Great Train Robbery of the Old West took place in the early 1870s, a period when train robberies were becoming increasingly common. The target of this particular heist was a train carrying a large shipment of gold and currency, bound for a bank in a major western city. The outlaws knew that this train would be heavily guarded, but they also knew that the potential rewards were immense.

The planning for the robbery was meticulous. The outlaws chose a remote and desolate stretch of track, far from any towns or law enforcement, where the train would be forced to slow down due to the difficult terrain. They timed the heist for the dead of night, when the cover of darkness would give them an advantage.

On the night of the robbery, the outlaws executed their plan with precision. They placed obstructions on the tracks to force the train to stop, then stormed the engine and passenger cars. The train's guards, though prepared for trouble, were quickly overwhelmed by the sheer number of robbers and the element of surprise. The outlaws disconnected the engine and the car containing the gold from the rest of the train, leaving the passengers and crew stranded in the middle of nowhere.

With the train's engine under their control, the robbers drove it a short distance down the track to a predetermined location, where they had set up horses for their escape. They forced the guards to open the safe containing the gold, then loaded the heavy sacks onto their horses. Within minutes, they were gone, disappearing into the night with a fortune in gold and cash.

The Aftermath: A Nation in Shock

The news of the Great Train Robbery spread like wildfire, shocking the nation. Train travel was supposed to be safe, and the idea that a group of outlaws could so easily overpower a well-guarded train shook the public's confidence in the railroads. The railroad companies, already facing challenges from the rugged terrain and the difficulties of maintaining their infrastructure, now had to contend with the threat of robbery.

In response, the railroads began to take measures to protect their shipments. They increased the number of guards on trains, reinforced the safes used to store valuable cargo, and even hired Pinkerton detectives to track down the outlaws responsible for the robberies. However, these measures were not always effective, and train robberies continued to be a problem in the years that followed.

The outlaws who carried out the Great Train Robbery were relentlessly pursued by law enforcement. The Pinkerton Detective Agency, in particular, took a leading role in the manhunt, using their extensive network of informants and agents to track the robbers across the frontier. Despite their efforts, however, many of the outlaws managed to evade capture, either disappearing into the wilderness or blending into the growing population of the western towns.

The Legend: The Making of Folk Heroes

The Great Train Robbery of the Old West quickly became a part of American folklore, with the outlaws involved in the heist being both feared and admired. Jesse James, in particular, was lionized by the press, which often portrayed him as a romantic figure—a brave rebel fighting against the establishment. This image was further bolstered by dime novels and other popular media of the time, which embellished the details of the robbery and cast the outlaws in a sympathetic light.

The reality, of course, was far different. The outlaws were hardened criminals who used violence and intimidation to achieve their goals, leaving a trail of victims in their wake. Many of the men involved in the

Great Train Robbery met violent ends, either killed in shootouts with lawmen or betrayed by their own associates.

Yet, the myth of the noble outlaw persisted, becoming a defining part of the cultural memory of the Old West. The Great Train Robbery came to symbolize the tension between law and lawlessness, civilization and the frontier, that defined the American West during this period.

The Lawmen: The Relentless Pursuit of Justice

The lawmen who pursued the outlaws responsible for the Great Train Robbery were also a key part of the story. These men were often as tough and resourceful as the criminals they hunted, driven by a sense of duty and a desire to bring justice to the lawless frontier.

Among the most famous of these lawmen were the Pinkerton detectives, who were hired by the railroad companies to track down the robbers. The Pinkertons were known for their relentless pursuit of criminals, using a combination of brute force and clever detective work to achieve their goals. They were feared by outlaws across the West, and their involvement in the manhunt for the Great Train Robbery only added to their reputation.

Other lawmen involved in the pursuit included local sheriffs and marshals, many of whom had deep ties to the communities they served. These men often worked in partnership with the Pinkertons, sharing information and resources to track down the robbers. The pursuit of the outlaws was dangerous and grueling work, requiring the lawmen to travel long distances through hostile territory and face off against heavily armed criminals.

Despite the challenges, the lawmen were eventually able to bring some of the outlaws to justice. Several members of the James-Younger Gang were captured or killed in the years following the robbery, while others went on to continue their criminal careers until they too met their end.

The Impact: The Changing Face of the West

The Great Train Robbery of the Old West had a lasting impact on the American West, influencing both the development of the region and the culture of the time. The robbery highlighted the challenges of maintaining law and order in a rapidly expanding frontier, where the forces of civilization were often at odds with the realities of life on the frontier.

In response to the robbery and other crimes of the era, the railroad companies and the government took steps to strengthen law enforcement in the West. New laws were passed to increase penalties for train robbery, and more resources were allocated to the pursuit of outlaws. These efforts helped to gradually bring the lawlessness of the frontier under control, paving the way for the eventual settlement and development of the West.

The cultural impact of the robbery was also significant. The story of the Great Train Robbery became a part of the mythology of the Old West, inspiring countless books, movies, and television shows. The image of the daring outlaw robbing a train in the dead of night became a staple of Western fiction, embodying the tension between freedom and order that defined the era.

The Legacy: A Symbol of the Wild West

Today, the Great Train Robbery of the Old West is remembered as one of the most iconic events in the history of the American frontier. It symbolizes the lawlessness and adventure of the Old West, a time when the boundaries between right and wrong were often blurred and the frontier was a place of both opportunity and danger.

The story of the robbery continues to captivate the imagination of people around the world, serving as a reminder of the complex and often contradictory nature of the American West. It is a tale of daring outlaws, determined lawmen, and a land in the midst of transformation—a story that, like the West itself, is both rugged and romantic, brutal and beautiful.

In the end, the Great Train Robbery of the Old West is more than just a historical event; it is a symbol of the enduring allure of the frontier, a place where anything was possible and where the line between legend and reality was often hard to discern. The robbery remains a defining moment in the history of the West, a testament to the enduring legacy of a time when the West was still wild and the possibilities seemed endless.

Chapter 4: The Billion-Dollar Bitcoin Heist

In the early 21st century, the world witnessed the birth of a revolutionary financial technology—cryptocurrency. Bitcoin, the first and most famous cryptocurrency, emerged in 2009, offering a decentralized and anonymous form of digital currency that quickly gained a dedicated following. Over the next decade, Bitcoin's value skyrocketed, attracting investors, tech enthusiasts, and eventually, criminals. The nature of Bitcoin, with its pseudonymous transactions and the difficulty of tracking it through traditional means, made it an attractive target for cybercriminals. Among the many stories of thefts and frauds in the world of cryptocurrency, one stands out as the most audacious and complex: The Billion-Dollar Bitcoin Heist.

The Background: Bitcoin and the Cryptographic Revolution

Bitcoin was created by an anonymous person or group of people using the pseudonym Satoshi Nakamoto. Its foundation lies in blockchain technology, a decentralized ledger that records all Bitcoin transactions across a network of computers. This technology ensured that Bitcoin transactions were secure, immutable, and transparent, yet the identities of those involved in the transactions remained hidden behind cryptographic addresses.

As Bitcoin gained popularity, its value began to rise, and by the mid-2010s, it had transformed from a niche digital currency into a mainstream financial asset. This meteoric rise in value made Bitcoin a prime target for cybercriminals. Exchanges—platforms where people could buy, sell, and trade Bitcoin—became particularly vulnerable. These exchanges held large amounts of Bitcoin in digital wallets, and the security of these wallets became a critical issue.

The Exchange: The Target of the Heist

The story of the Billion-Dollar Bitcoin Heist centers around one of the largest and most prominent cryptocurrency exchanges in the world: Bitfinex. Launched in 2012, Bitfinex quickly grew to become one of the leading exchanges for trading Bitcoin and other cryptocurrencies. It offered advanced trading features, high liquidity, and was trusted by millions of users worldwide.

However, the rapid growth of Bitfinex also made it a target. By 2016, the exchange was handling billions of dollars' worth of transactions, making it one of the most lucrative targets for cybercriminals. The exchange's security infrastructure was robust, but it was not infallible. Cybercriminals were constantly probing for weaknesses, and in August 2016, they found one.

The Heist: A Coordinated and Calculated Attack

The Billion-Dollar Bitcoin Heist was not the result of a single breach or flaw but rather a series of coordinated and highly sophisticated attacks that exploited vulnerabilities in Bitfinex's security protocols. The attackers targeted the multi-signature wallets used by Bitfinex to store users' Bitcoin. These wallets required multiple keys to authorize a transaction, a feature designed to enhance security by ensuring that no single point of failure could compromise the funds.

However, the attackers discovered a vulnerability in the system used by Bitfinex to manage these multi-signature wallets. By exploiting this flaw, they were able to bypass the multi-signature requirement and initiate unauthorized withdrawals. Over the course of the attack, which went undetected for several hours, the hackers were able to siphon off approximately 120,000 Bitcoin from Bitfinex's wallets.

At the time of the theft, the stolen Bitcoin was worth around $72 million. However, as Bitcoin's value continued to rise in the years following the heist, the value of the stolen coins eventually exceeded $1 billion, making it one of the largest and most significant thefts in the history of cryptocurrency.

The Aftermath: Shockwaves Through the Crypto World

The revelation of the Billion-Dollar Bitcoin Heist sent shockwaves through the cryptocurrency community and the broader financial world. The news of the breach caused a massive sell-off in Bitcoin and other cryptocurrencies, leading to a sharp drop in prices. Bitfinex temporarily suspended trading and withdrawals as it scrambled to contain the damage and assess the full extent of the breach.

For the users of Bitfinex, the heist was a disaster. Thousands of individuals had their Bitcoin holdings stolen, and the exchange faced immense pressure to make its users whole. To address the situation, Bitfinex took the unprecedented step of issuing "BFX tokens" to its users, representing the value of the stolen Bitcoin. These tokens could be traded on the exchange or redeemed at a later date if Bitfinex was able to recover the stolen funds.

Bitfinex also implemented a recovery plan that involved gradually repurchasing the BFX tokens from users, a process that took several months. Remarkably, by April 2017, Bitfinex had fully repaid all of its users, a move that helped restore some confidence in the exchange. However, the damage to its reputation was significant, and the incident highlighted the risks and challenges associated with the rapidly evolving world of cryptocurrency.

The Investigation: The Hunt for the Perpetrators

Following the heist, law enforcement agencies, cybersecurity experts, and independent investigators launched an extensive investigation to track down the perpetrators and recover the stolen Bitcoin. The anonymous and decentralized nature of Bitcoin made this task extraordinarily difficult. The stolen Bitcoin was moved through a complex web of transactions across multiple addresses, making it challenging to trace the funds to a specific individual or group.

One of the key challenges in the investigation was the use of mixing services, also known as tumblers, by the attackers. These services allow users to mix their Bitcoin with others, effectively obfuscating the trail and making it nearly impossible to trace the origin of the funds. The attackers utilized these services to launder the stolen Bitcoin, further complicating the efforts to track the funds.

Despite these obstacles, investigators made some progress. Over the years, small amounts of the stolen Bitcoin were traced and recovered, often as a result of mistakes made by the attackers or through the cooperation of cryptocurrency exchanges. However, the vast majority of the stolen Bitcoin remained elusive, locked away in digital wallets whose owners could not be identified.

In 2022, a significant breakthrough occurred when U.S. law enforcement agencies announced the arrest of a couple, Ilya Lichtenstein and Heather Morgan, in connection with the 2016 Bitfinex hack. The authorities seized over $3.6 billion worth of Bitcoin from wallets associated with the couple, making it one of the largest financial seizures in U.S. history. The couple was accused of conspiring to launder the stolen Bitcoin, but the full details of their involvement and whether they were the original hackers remained unclear.

The Legal and Ethical Implications: A New Frontier of Crime

The Billion-Dollar Bitcoin Heist raised significant legal and ethical questions about the nature of digital currency, the responsibilities of exchanges, and the role of law enforcement in the digital age. The anonymous and borderless nature of Bitcoin made it a unique challenge for regulators and law enforcement agencies, who were often ill-equipped to deal with such crimes.

One of the key issues was the question of jurisdiction. The global nature of cryptocurrency transactions meant that the perpetrators could be located anywhere in the world, making it difficult for any single country to take effective action. This led to calls for greater international cooperation and the development of new legal frameworks to address the challenges posed by digital currencies.

Another important issue was the responsibility of cryptocurrency exchanges to protect their users' funds. The Bitfinex heist exposed the vulnerabilities in the security protocols used by exchanges and highlighted the need for more robust measures to protect against cyberattacks. In the years following the heist, many exchanges implemented stronger security practices, such as cold storage (keeping funds offline), enhanced encryption, and multi-factor authentication.

The ethical implications of the heist were also significant. The pseudonymous nature of Bitcoin transactions meant that individuals and organizations could potentially engage in illegal activities without fear of detection. This raised concerns about the use of cryptocurrency for money laundering, terrorist financing, and other criminal activities. The Bitfinex heist became a symbol of the darker side of the cryptocurrency revolution, serving as a reminder of the risks and challenges associated with the new digital economy.

The Impact on the Cryptocurrency Market: A Turning Point

The Billion-Dollar Bitcoin Heist was a watershed moment for the cryptocurrency market. The scale of the theft and the subsequent market turmoil underscored the volatility and risks inherent in the emerging digital currency ecosystem. For many investors, the heist was a wake-up call, highlighting the need for greater caution and due diligence when dealing with cryptocurrencies.

In the wake of the heist, there was a renewed focus on security within the cryptocurrency industry. Exchanges and other cryptocurrency-related businesses began to prioritize the implementation of more advanced security measures to protect their platforms and users. This included the adoption of multi-signature wallets, cold storage solutions, and improved monitoring and auditing practices.

The heist also had a lasting impact on the regulatory landscape. Governments and financial regulators around the world began to take a closer look at the cryptocurrency industry, leading to the development of new regulations aimed at preventing similar incidents in the future. These regulations often focused on the need for exchanges to implement strong security protocols, conduct thorough know-your-customer (KYC) and anti-money laundering (AML) procedures, and cooperate with law enforcement in the event of a breach.

Despite the negative impact of the heist, the cryptocurrency market continued to grow in the years that followed. Bitcoin and other cryptocurrencies became more widely accepted as investment assets, and the market matured with the introduction of new financial products, such as futures contracts and exchange-traded funds (ETFs). However, the memory of the Billion-Dollar Bitcoin Heist remained, serving as a cautionary tale for investors and businesses alike.

The Legacy: A Cautionary Tale for the Digital Age

The Billion-Dollar Bitcoin Heist has become one of the most infamous events in the history of cryptocurrency, a story of greed, ingenuity, and the challenges of a rapidly evolving digital landscape. It serves as a stark reminder of the risks associated with digital currencies and the importance of security in the digital age.

For the cryptocurrency industry, the heist was a turning point that led to increased scrutiny, improved security measures, and a greater awareness of the vulnerabilities inherent in the digital economy. It also highlighted the need for stronger international cooperation and regulatory frameworks to address the unique challenges posed by cryptocurrencies.

For the broader public, the heist became a symbol of the potential dangers of the digital revolution. As more aspects of our lives become digitized, the risk of cybercrime grows, and the Billion-Dollar Bitcoin Heist serves as a reminder that even the most advanced technologies are not immune to exploitation.

In the years since the heist, the world of cryptocurrency has continued to evolve, with new innovations, challenges, and opportunities emerging on a regular basis. Yet, the story of the Billion-Dollar Bitcoin Heist remains a powerful and enduring narrative, a testament to the complexities and contradictions of the digital age. It is a story that will likely be told for years to come, a modern-day legend that encapsulates the promise and peril of the new frontier of finance.

Chapter 5: The Heist at Sea: Pirate Plunder

Throughout history, the vast oceans have been both a highway of commerce and a lawless frontier where the rule of law was often supplanted by the rule of the strongest. The seas have witnessed countless tales of adventure, exploration, and conquest, but none are as thrilling or as feared as the tales of piracy. The Age of Piracy, which spanned from the late 17th to the early 18th century, is often romanticized in popular culture. However, behind the swashbuckling legends lies a brutal reality of violence, betrayal, and greed. Among the many stories of piracy, the "Heist at Sea" stands out as one of the most audacious and treacherous acts of plunder ever recorded.

The Golden Age of Piracy: Context and Background

To fully understand the significance of the Heist at Sea, it is essential to delve into the era known as the Golden Age of Piracy. This period, roughly between 1650 and 1730, was marked by an explosion of pirate activity in the Caribbean, the Atlantic, and the Indian Ocean. The decline of European empires, the end of major wars, and the increased volume of maritime trade created the perfect conditions for piracy to flourish.

Pirates, often former sailors or privateers left unemployed by the end of conflicts, turned to piracy as a means of survival and wealth acquisition. They preyed on merchant vessels, raiding their holds for valuable cargo such as gold, silver, spices, and other goods. Some pirates became infamous, their names echoing through history—Blackbeard, Captain Kidd, Anne Bonny, and Bartholomew Roberts, to name a few. These pirates operated with impunity, their ships prowling the seas, striking fear into the hearts of sailors and merchants alike.

The Target: A Treasure-Laden Galleon

The story of the Heist at Sea revolves around a treasure-laden galleon, a type of large sailing ship used primarily by European powers, especially the Spanish, during the Age of Exploration. These galleons were the workhorses of the maritime empires, transporting vast amounts of wealth from the colonies back to Europe. They were heavily armed but also heavily burdened with treasure, making them both a prize and a challenge for any pirate crew.

The galleon in question was the Nuestra Señora de la Concepción, one of the most heavily guarded treasure ships in the Spanish fleet. It was tasked with transporting a fortune in gold, silver, and precious gems from the New World back to Spain. The ship's hold was filled with the spoils of the Americas—bars of gold and silver from the mines of Peru, chests of emeralds and diamonds, and bags of coins minted from the riches of the colonies. The Concepción was a floating treasure trove, and its journey across the Atlantic was one fraught with danger.

The Plot: A Perfect Storm of Opportunity and Deception

The Heist at Sea was not a spur-of-the-moment attack but a carefully planned and meticulously executed operation. The plot was the brainchild of a notorious pirate captain known only by his feared moniker, "El Diablo." El Diablo was a master of deception and strategy, known for his cunning and ruthlessness. He had spent years gathering intelligence on the Spanish treasure fleets, learning their routes, schedules, and defenses.

El Diablo knew that attacking a heavily armed galleon like the Concepción head-on would be suicidal. Instead, he devised a plan that involved deception, betrayal, and a perfect understanding of the sea's unpredictable nature. His crew consisted of seasoned pirates, men who had been with him through countless battles and who knew the risks and rewards of the life they had chosen.

The first step in the plot was to create a ruse that would lure the Concepción into a vulnerable position. El Diablo had spies within the Spanish colonies who provided him with detailed information about the galleon's departure and its expected route. Armed with this knowledge, he set his plan into motion.

El Diablo and his crew sailed their ship, the Devil's Advocate, to a remote island in the Caribbean, where they staged a mock shipwreck. They beached their ship on a reef and set up a distress signal, knowing that the Concepción, like any other ship, would be compelled by maritime law and custom to assist a vessel in distress. The Devil's Advocate was strategically positioned near a narrow strait, a natural chokepoint that would leave the Concepción vulnerable to attack.

The Encounter: A Fatal Mistake

As the Concepción approached the island, the captain of the galleon, Don Rodrigo, spotted the distress signal. Unaware of the trap that lay ahead, he ordered the ship to alter course and offer assistance to the stranded vessel. The crew of the Concepción had no reason to suspect foul play; after all, the sea was a dangerous place, and shipwrecks were common.

As the Concepción drew closer to the Devil's Advocate, the pirates sprang their trap. Hidden below decks and in the rigging, El Diablo's men waited for the signal to attack. When the Concepción was within range, El Diablo himself gave the order. The pirates emerged from their hiding places and unleashed a devastating broadside of cannon fire on the unsuspecting galleon.

The Concepción was caught completely off guard. The pirates' cannons tore through the ship's hull, shattering its masts and rigging. The galleon, weighed down by its treasure, was slow to maneuver, and within minutes, it was at the mercy of the pirates. The crew of the Concepción fought valiantly, but they were no match for the experienced and bloodthirsty pirates.

The Boarding: A Battle for Treasure

With the Concepción disabled, the pirates boarded the galleon, cutting down anyone who stood in their way. The battle on the decks was fierce and bloody, with swords clashing and pistols firing in the chaos. Don Rodrigo, the captain of the Concepción, was determined to protect his ship and its treasure, but he was outnumbered and outmatched.

El Diablo himself led the boarding party, cutting a path through the defenders with his cutlass. He reached the captain's quarters, where Don Rodrigo made his last stand. The two men fought a brutal duel, but in the end, El Diablo's skill and ferocity won out. Don Rodrigo fell, and with his death, the last resistance on the Concepción crumbled.

The pirates quickly secured the ship, rounding up the surviving crew members and forcing them to reveal the location of the treasure. The Concepción's hold was packed with gold, silver, and jewels, more wealth than any of the pirates had ever seen. The plunder was beyond their wildest dreams, a fortune that could set them up for life.

The Escape: A Race Against Time

With the treasure secured, El Diablo knew that time was of the essence. The Spanish navy would soon be on their trail, and they had to move quickly to avoid capture. The pirates transferred the treasure from the Concepción to the Devil's Advocate, working day and night to load the chests of gold and silver onto their ship.

As they worked, the weather began to turn. A storm was brewing on the horizon, and the sea, which had been their ally in the heist, now threatened to become their enemy. The pirates finished loading the treasure just as the first signs of the storm appeared—dark clouds gathering in the sky and the wind beginning to howl.

El Diablo ordered his crew to set sail, leaving the Concepción to sink with its remaining crew members still aboard. The Devil's Advocate, now heavily laden with treasure, struggled to make headway against the rising seas. The storm hit with full force, and the ship was tossed about by the waves, its sails torn and its masts creaking under the strain.

Despite the ferocity of the storm, El Diablo's skill as a captain saw them through. He steered the ship with a steady hand, navigating through the treacherous waters as the storm raged around them. After hours of battling the elements, the Devil's Advocate finally emerged from the storm, battered but still afloat.

The Aftermath: A Fortune and a Legend

The Heist at Sea was a resounding success for El Diablo and his crew. They had pulled off one of the most daring and lucrative acts of piracy in history, stealing a fortune that would make them legends. The treasure was hidden on a remote island, where the pirates divided it among themselves according to the pirate code.

El Diablo's share of the loot was enormous, enough to retire on and live a life of luxury. But for a man like El Diablo, the thrill of the sea and the allure of the next big score were too powerful to resist. Rather than retire, he continued his life of piracy, becoming even more feared and infamous as the years went on.

The Spanish authorities were furious at the loss of the Concepción and its treasure. They launched a massive manhunt for El Diablo and his crew, but the pirates were always one step ahead, using their knowledge of the sea and their network of informants to stay out of reach. Despite the best efforts of the Spanish navy, El Diablo was never captured, and the treasure of the Concepción was never recovered.

The Legacy: The Enduring Myth of Pirate Treasure

The Heist at Sea became one of the most famous stories of the Golden Age of Piracy, a tale of audacity, cunning, and ruthless ambition. It embodied the spirit of the pirate—lawless, fearless, and driven by the pursuit of wealth and freedom. The story of the heist was passed down through generations, becoming part of the rich folklore of the sea.

The legend of the treasure of the Concepción persisted long after the Golden Age of Piracy had ended. Treasure hunters and adventurers searched for the lost hoard, lured by the promise of untold riches. Some claimed to have found clues to the treasure's location, while others spent their lives chasing a dream that always seemed just out of reach.

In popular culture, the Heist at Sea has been romanticized and retold in countless books, movies, and television shows. It captures the imagination of people around the world, symbolizing the enduring fascination with pirates and the mysteries of the sea. The story of the heist serves as a reminder of the dangers and rewards of life on the high seas, a world where fortune favors the bold, and where the line between hero and villain is often blurred.

Conclusion: A Timeless Tale of Adventure and Greed

The Heist at Sea: Pirate Plunder is more than just a story of theft; it is a narrative that encapsulates the essence of piracy during the Golden Age. It is a tale of adventure, cunning, and greed, set against the backdrop of the vast and unforgiving ocean. The heist is a testament to the audacity and ruthlessness of the pirates who roamed the seas, defying the powers of their time and carving out their own destiny.

As we look back on this era, the Heist at Sea remains one of the most compelling and enduring stories of piracy. It serves as a reminder of the human capacity for both great evil and great daring, and it continues to captivate those who are drawn to the romance and danger of the high seas. In the annals of pirate history, the Heist at Sea will always stand as a defining moment, a tale that echoes through time and continues to inspire new generations of adventurers and storytellers.

Chapter 6: The Great Bourbon Barrel Burglary

Bourbon is more than just a type of whiskey; it is a symbol of American heritage, deeply rooted in the culture and history of Kentucky. Often referred to as "America's Native Spirit," bourbon has been crafted in the United States since the late 18th century. It has grown from humble beginnings in small distilleries to become a globally recognized and highly prized spirit, known for its rich flavor and unique production process.

The production of bourbon is a meticulous art that involves the careful selection of grains, the aging process in charred oak barrels, and the specific requirements set by law. By definition, bourbon must be made from at least 51% corn, aged in new charred oak barrels, and distilled to no more than 160 proof. These stringent regulations ensure that each bottle of bourbon meets the high standards that have made it a beloved drink worldwide.

Kentucky, with its limestone-rich water, fertile soil, and ideal climate for aging, is the heart of bourbon production. Over 95% of the world's bourbon is produced in the Bluegrass State, and the industry is a vital part of the local economy. The rolling hills of Kentucky are dotted with distilleries, many of which have been in operation for generations, contributing to the state's reputation as the birthplace of bourbon.

However, the popularity and value of bourbon have also made it a target for criminals. The Great Bourbon Barrel Burglary, one of the most audacious thefts in recent memory, shook the bourbon industry to its core. This heist involved not just the theft of a few bottles, but entire barrels of aging bourbon—a crime that highlighted the lengths to which some would go to get their hands on this liquid gold.

The Background: Bourbon's Rising Value and the Birth of the Heist

In recent years, bourbon has experienced a resurgence in popularity, both in the United States and abroad. Collectors and connoisseurs alike have driven up demand for rare and aged bourbons, with some bottles fetching thousands of dollars at auction. Limited-edition releases and older vintages have become particularly coveted, and the secondary market for bourbon has flourished. This boom in popularity has made bourbon not just a drink, but an investment.

As bourbon's value skyrocketed, so too did the temptation for those looking to make a quick profit. Distilleries took notice of the growing black market, where barrels and bottles could be sold for significant sums without the oversight of regulatory bodies. This underground trade created an opportunity for those willing to exploit the system, leading to a rise in thefts from distilleries and warehouses across Kentucky.

The Great Bourbon Barrel Burglary stands out as one of the most significant of these crimes, not only because of the scale of the theft but also because of the people involved and the sophisticated nature of the operation. This heist was not the work of a few opportunistic thieves; it was a coordinated effort by individuals with inside knowledge and a deep understanding of the bourbon industry.

The Players: An Inside Job

The mastermind behind the Great Bourbon Barrel Burglary was none other than Gilbert "Toby" Curtsinger, a long-time employee of the Wild Turkey distillery. Curtsinger, who had worked in the bourbon industry for over a decade, knew the ins and outs of the production process, the layout of the distilleries, and the security measures in place. This knowledge gave him a significant advantage in planning and executing the heist.

Curtsinger was not working alone. He assembled a small but trusted crew, many of whom were also employees of the distilleries or had connections within the bourbon industry. This network of insiders allowed Curtsinger to orchestrate the theft without raising suspicion. They had access to the warehouses, knew when security was lax, and understood how to move the barrels without drawing attention.

The plan was simple in concept but complex in execution: over several years, Curtsinger and his crew would steal barrels of bourbon directly from the distilleries, as well as rare and valuable bottles from private collections. The stolen bourbon would then be sold on the black market, where collectors and buyers, eager to acquire rare vintages, were willing to pay top dollar without asking too many questions about the origins of the whiskey.

The Execution: How the Bourbon Was Stolen

The thefts began gradually, with Curtsinger and his crew pilfering barrels from warehouses during their shifts. The barrels, which typically weigh around 500 pounds when full, were not easy to move, but the thieves had access to forklifts and trucks, making the task manageable. They would load the barrels onto trucks and transport them to Curtsinger's property, where they were stored until buyers could be found.

The stolen barrels were often older, more valuable bourbons—some of which were destined for limited-edition releases or special bottlings. Curtsinger knew exactly which barrels to target, selecting those that would fetch the highest prices on the black market. Over time, the scale of the operation grew, with more barrels disappearing from the warehouses and more bottles being stolen from private collections.

The crew also targeted specific brands known for their high value, including Pappy Van Winkle, one of the most sought-after bourbons in the world. Pappy Van Winkle's Family Reserve is legendary among bourbon enthusiasts, with older vintages selling for thousands of dollars per bottle. The theft of even a few bottles of Pappy could result in a significant payday for the thieves.

Curtsinger's crew was careful to avoid detection. They spread out the thefts over several years, taking only a few barrels or bottles at a time to avoid drawing attention. The stolen bourbon was sold quietly through word-of-mouth networks, with buyers often unaware that they were purchasing stolen goods. The thieves also used connections within the bourbon community to find willing buyers, further insulating themselves from the risk of exposure.

The Discovery: The Cracks in the Plan

For years, the thefts went unnoticed. The bourbon industry, while growing, was still somewhat insular, and the distilleries did not immediately realize the extent of the losses. However, as more barrels and bottles went missing, and as the black market for rare bourbons continued to thrive, rumors began to circulate.

The first significant break in the case came when a tip-off alerted authorities to the possibility of stolen bourbon being sold on the black market. This tip, combined with an increase in theft reports from distilleries, led to an investigation by the Franklin County Sheriff's Office in Kentucky. The investigation was codenamed "Operation Bourbon Trail," and it focused on uncovering the extent of the thefts and identifying those responsible.

The investigation revealed a complex web of transactions and connections within the bourbon community. As authorities dug deeper, they began to piece together the scale of the operation and the involvement of Curtsinger and his crew. Surveillance, interviews, and forensic evidence slowly built the case against the thieves, culminating in a series of raids and arrests.

The Raid: Bringing the Thieves to Justice

In March 2015, authorities executed a series of search warrants that led to the discovery of several barrels of stolen bourbon on Curtsinger's property. The raid was the culmination of months of investigation, and it confirmed the suspicions of the investigators. The barrels, some of which were marked with the distinctive logos of the distilleries, provided the concrete evidence needed to charge Curtsinger and his accomplices.

Curtsinger was arrested and charged with multiple felonies, including theft by unlawful taking, receiving stolen property, and engaging in organized crime. Several of his accomplices were also arrested and charged in connection with the thefts. The arrests sent shockwaves through the bourbon industry, as the extent of the operation became clear.

In the aftermath of the raid, authorities seized more than $100,000 worth of stolen bourbon, including barrels of Wild Turkey and Buffalo Trace, as well as rare bottles of Pappy Van Winkle. The recovery of the stolen bourbon was a significant victory for law enforcement, but it also highlighted the vulnerability of the industry to such crimes.

The Trial: A Cautionary Tale for the Bourbon Industry

The trial of Gilbert "Toby" Curtsinger and his accomplices was closely watched by the bourbon industry and the public. It was a cautionary tale about the lengths to which people would go to profit from the bourbon boom. During the trial, Curtsinger admitted to his role in the thefts, detailing how he had used his insider knowledge to orchestrate the heist.

In a plea agreement, Curtsinger was sentenced to 15 years in prison, though he would be eligible for parole after serving a portion of his sentence. Several of his accomplices also received prison sentences, and the case served as a warning to others who might consider similar crimes.

The Great Bourbon Barrel Burglary forced the bourbon industry to reevaluate its security measures. Distilleries implemented stricter controls over access to their warehouses, increased surveillance, and took steps to better track their inventory. The case also prompted discussions about the need for more robust oversight of the secondary market for bourbon, where stolen goods could easily be sold to unsuspecting buyers.

The Legacy: The Impact of the Heist on the Bourbon Industry

The Great Bourbon Barrel Burglary had a lasting impact on the bourbon industry. It exposed vulnerabilities in the way distilleries managed and protected their valuable products and highlighted the need for greater collaboration between law enforcement and the industry to prevent future thefts.

In the years following the heist, the bourbon industry continued to grow, with Kentucky's distilleries producing more bourbon than ever before. The demand for rare and aged bourbons showed no signs of slowing, and the secondary market remained active. However, the lessons learned from the heist led to improved security measures and a greater awareness of the risks associated with the industry's booming popularity.

The heist also became part of bourbon lore, a story that would be retold in books, documentaries, and news articles. It serves as a reminder of the dark side of the bourbon boom and the lengths to which some will go to profit from the industry's success. The tale of the Great Bourbon

Barrel Burglary is now etched into the history of Kentucky bourbon, a chapter that underscores the value and allure of America's Native Spirit.

Conclusion: A Cautionary Tale of Greed and Consequence

The Great Bourbon Barrel Burglary is a story of ambition, greed, and the consequences of crossing the line between opportunity and crime. It is a tale that resonates beyond the bourbon industry, offering a glimpse into the human desire for wealth and the lengths to which some will go to obtain it. For the bourbon industry, the heist was a wake-up call, leading to lasting changes that have helped protect the integrity of Kentucky's most famous product.

As the bourbon industry continues to thrive, the memory of the heist serves as both a cautionary tale and a testament to the enduring appeal of bourbon. The Great Bourbon Barrel Burglary will be remembered not just for the audacity of the crime, but for the way it brought to light the challenges and vulnerabilities faced by an industry that produces one of the world's most beloved spirits.

Chapter 7: The Infiltration of Fort Knox

Fort Knox, the United States Bullion Depository, is synonymous with impenetrability and wealth. Located in Kentucky, it houses a significant portion of the United States' gold reserves and has long been a symbol of national security. The very notion of infiltrating Fort Knox is the stuff of legend, conspiracy theories, and Hollywood blockbusters. But what if someone actually attempted it? What if the most secure vault in the world was at risk? This comprehensive exploration will delve into the history of Fort Knox, its significance, security measures, and the myths and realities surrounding potential infiltration attempts.

The Origins of Fort Knox

Fort Knox's story begins in the midst of the Great Depression, a time of economic uncertainty and fluctuating gold prices. The United States government, seeking to stabilize its economy, passed the Gold Reserve Act of 1934, which required all gold to be turned over to the U.S. Treasury. This led to the need for a secure facility to store the nation's gold reserves.

In 1936, construction of the United States Bullion Depository began within the Fort Knox military base, a location chosen for its remote yet accessible position, as well as its existing military protection. The structure was completed in December 1936, and by 1937, the first shipments of gold arrived. The vault was constructed with one goal in mind: to be impenetrable. With walls made of granite, concrete, and steel, and a door weighing over 20 tons, Fort Knox was built to withstand any conceivable threat.

The Role of Fort Knox in American History

Beyond being a repository for gold, Fort Knox has played a significant role in American history. During World War II, it housed the original

Declaration of Independence, the Constitution, and the Bill of Rights, as well as other priceless artifacts, to protect them from potential threats. It also served as a training ground for soldiers, particularly armored divisions, due to its vast, rugged terrain.

Fort Knox has come to symbolize American financial stability and strength. The gold stored within its walls represents a significant portion of the nation's reserves, although the exact amount has been the subject of speculation and debate for decades. Over the years, Fort Knox has become the subject of numerous conspiracy theories, with some questioning whether the gold is even there at all, and others suggesting that it has been secretly moved or stolen.

Security Measures: The Impenetrable Fortress

Fort Knox is widely regarded as one of the most secure places on Earth. The security measures in place are designed to thwart any infiltration attempts, no matter how sophisticated. While the exact details of Fort Knox's security are classified, a combination of physical barriers, technological defenses, and military protection ensures that the facility remains impenetrable.

- **Physical Security**

The structure of Fort Knox itself is a formidable barrier to any would-be infiltrators. The building is constructed from 16,000 cubic feet of granite, 4,200 cubic yards of concrete, 750 tons of reinforced steel, and 670 tons of structural steel. The vault door, which weighs over 20 tons, is secured by a lock so complex that no single person knows the entire combination. Instead, several individuals must work together to unlock it, adding another layer of security.

The building is surrounded by multiple layers of security, including fences topped with barbed wire, minefields, and a moat. The area around Fort Knox is a military base, patrolled by armed guards, tanks, and helicopters. The airspace above the depository is a no-fly zone, and the surrounding area is heavily monitored by surveillance cameras and sensors designed to detect any unauthorized entry.

- **Technological Defenses**

In addition to its physical barriers, Fort Knox is equipped with advanced technological defenses. These include motion detectors, infrared cameras, and seismic sensors capable of detecting even the slightest movement. The facility is also equipped with electronic jamming devices to prevent the use of remote-controlled devices or communications equipment by potential infiltrators.

The depository's security systems are designed to be redundant, with multiple backup systems in place to ensure that a breach in one area does not compromise the entire facility. These systems are constantly updated to incorporate the latest advancements in security technology.

- **Military Protection**

Fort Knox's location within a military base provides an additional layer of security. The base is home to a detachment of the United States Mint Police, a federal law enforcement agency responsible for protecting the nation's gold reserves. These highly trained officers are equipped with the latest weapons and technology to respond to any threat.

In addition to the Mint Police, Fort Knox is protected by the United States Army, which maintains a significant presence on the base. Tanks, armored vehicles, and attack helicopters are stationed at Fort Knox, ready to respond to any attempt at infiltration. The base also has its own rapid response force, which can be deployed within minutes to deal with any security breach.

Myths and Legends: The Conspiracy Theories Surrounding Fort Knox

Given its status as a symbol of American financial power and security, it's no surprise that Fort Knox has become the subject of numerous conspiracy theories and legends. Some of these theories are based on historical events, while others are purely speculative.

- **The "Empty Vault" Theory**

One of the most persistent conspiracy theories surrounding Fort Knox is the idea that the vault is empty or contains far less gold than officially claimed. This theory gained traction in the 1970s when U.S. Representative Ron Paul and others called for an audit of the nation's gold reserves. Despite assurances from the U.S. Treasury that the gold is accounted for, the lack of a comprehensive, independent audit has fueled speculation that the gold has been secretly sold or removed.

Proponents of the "empty vault" theory often point to the fact that Fort Knox has not been opened to public inspection since 1974 when a group of journalists and congressmen were allowed a brief, highly controlled visit. Skeptics argue that this lack of transparency is evidence that the government is hiding something, although there is no concrete proof to support this claim.

- **The Nazi Gold Conspiracy**

Another popular conspiracy theory involves the idea that Fort Knox contains not just U.S. gold reserves but also looted Nazi gold. According to this theory, during and after World War II, the U.S. government secretly transported gold stolen by the Nazis from occupied countries to Fort Knox. This gold, it is claimed, was never returned to its rightful owners and remains hidden in the vaults of the depository.

While there is historical evidence that the U.S. and other Allied nations recovered gold stolen by the Nazis, there is no credible evidence to support the claim that this gold was secretly moved to Fort Knox. Nevertheless, the idea of hidden Nazi gold has captured the imagination of conspiracy theorists and continues to be a popular topic of speculation.

- **The Secret Infiltration Attempts**

Over the years, there have been rumors of secret infiltration attempts on Fort Knox, often involving elite foreign agents or rogue elements within the U.S. government. These stories typically involve elaborate plots to steal the gold or sabotage the depository, often with the goal of destabilizing the U.S. economy or funding covert operations.

One such story involves a supposed plot by Soviet spies during the Cold War to infiltrate Fort Knox and steal gold to finance communist movements around the world. According to this tale, the plot was foiled by U.S. intelligence agencies, who intercepted the spies before they could reach the depository. While there is no evidence to support this story, it has become a popular part of Fort Knox lore.

Hollywood and Pop Culture: Fort Knox in the Public Imagination

The idea of infiltrating Fort Knox has long been a popular theme in Hollywood and pop culture. Movies, television shows, and books have all explored the concept, often portraying Fort Knox as the ultimate challenge for master thieves, spies, or action heroes.

- **"Goldfinger" (1964)**

One of the most famous portrayals of Fort Knox in popular culture is in the 1964 James Bond film "Goldfinger." In the movie, the villain Auric Goldfinger devises a plan to infiltrate Fort Knox and detonate a nuclear bomb inside the vault, contaminating the U.S. gold reserves and increasing the value of his own gold holdings.

The film's depiction of Fort Knox, with its vast underground vaults and gold bars stacked to the ceiling, is highly fictionalized. However, "Goldfinger" has left a lasting impact on the public's perception of Fort Knox and has contributed to the enduring fascination with the idea of infiltrating the depository.

- **"Die Hard with a Vengeance" (1995)**

Another popular film that explores the idea of infiltrating Fort Knox is "Die Hard with a Vengeance." In the movie, the villain Simon Gruber, played by Jeremy Irons, orchestrates a complex heist to steal gold from the Federal Reserve Bank in New York City, but his plan ultimately involves misdirecting authorities to Fort Knox as part of his scheme.

While Fort Knox is not the primary focus of the film, its mention underscores its status as the ultimate symbol of wealth and security. The film plays on the idea that Fort Knox is so well-protected that even a seasoned criminal mastermind would hesitate to target it directly.

- **Other Depictions**

Fort Knox has appeared in various other films, television shows, and books, often as a backdrop for action-packed heists or daring infiltration attempts. These portrayals have contributed to the mystique surrounding Fort Knox and have reinforced its reputation as an impenetrable fortress.

The Realities of Infiltrating Fort Knox: Is It Even Possible?

While the idea of infiltrating Fort Knox makes for compelling fiction, the reality is far less glamorous. The security measures in place at Fort

Knox are designed to prevent any unauthorized access, and the consequences of attempting to breach the facility would be severe.

- **The Challenges of Infiltration**

The physical and technological defenses at Fort Knox present a formidable challenge to anyone attempting to infiltrate the facility. The vault is buried deep within the depository, protected by layers of granite, concrete, and steel. Even if an infiltrator managed to breach the outer defenses, they would still need to bypass the vault door, which requires multiple people to open.

The surrounding military base adds another layer of difficulty, with armed guards, tanks, and helicopters ready to respond to any threat. The area is heavily monitored by surveillance cameras and sensors, and the airspace above Fort Knox is a no-fly zone.

Infiltrators would also need to contend with the advanced technological defenses in place, including motion detectors, infrared cameras, and electronic jamming devices. Even if they managed to evade detection, the redundant security systems would likely trigger an alarm, alerting the authorities to their presence.

- **The Legal and Ethical Implications**

Beyond the practical challenges, there are significant legal and ethical implications to consider. Infiltrating Fort Knox would be a federal crime, punishable by severe penalties, including long prison sentences. The U.S. government takes the security of its gold reserves very seriously, and any attempt to breach Fort Knox would be met with a swift and forceful response.

There are also ethical considerations to take into account. Stealing from Fort Knox would not only be a crime but also an attack on the financial stability of the United States. The gold stored at Fort Knox represents a significant portion of the nation's reserves, and any theft or damage to the depository could have serious economic consequences.

Conclusion: The Legacy of Fort Knox

Fort Knox remains one of the most secure and mysterious places in the world. Its impenetrability has made it the subject of countless myths, legends, and conspiracy theories, but the reality is that infiltrating Fort Knox is virtually impossible. The combination of physical, technological, and military defenses ensures that the U.S. gold reserves are well-protected, and any attempt to breach the facility would be met with overwhelming force.

While the idea of infiltrating Fort Knox will likely continue to capture the public's imagination, the true legacy of the depository lies in its role as a symbol of American strength and security. The gold stored within its walls represents not just wealth, but the nation's commitment to protecting its financial stability and safeguarding its future.

Chapter 8: The Great Art Heist of the Louvre

The Louvre Museum in Paris is not just a repository of some of the world's greatest art but also a symbol of human achievement, cultural history, and artistic excellence. Housing over 38,000 works of art, including the famed Mona Lisa and the Venus de Milo, it is the largest and most visited museum in the world. The Louvre's reputation as a fortress of artistic treasures, however, makes it an irresistible target for audacious criminals. Among the many tales of theft and intrigue associated with the Louvre, one stands out as particularly audacious and enigmatic: The Great Art Heist of the Louvre.

This heist is not just a tale of stolen art; it is a story that delves deep into the psyche of those who dared to challenge one of the most secure and respected institutions in the world. It is a saga of ambition, greed, and cunning, intertwined with the mysteries of art that have fascinated humanity for centuries. This detailed exploration will take you through the history of the Louvre, the significance of the stolen art, the meticulous planning behind the heist, the aftermath, and the lingering questions that remain unanswered to this day.

The Louvre: A Bastion of Art and History

- **A Brief History of the Louvre**

The Louvre's origins date back to the late 12th century when it was originally constructed as a fortress by King Philip II to protect Paris from potential invasions. Over the centuries, it was transformed from a military stronghold to a royal palace, and finally, after the French Revolution, into a public museum in 1793. Today, the Louvre is a sprawling complex of buildings that has undergone numerous expansions and renovations, reflecting the architectural and cultural evolution of France.

The museum's collection spans over 9,000 years, from ancient civilizations to the 19th century, encompassing a vast array of artistic disciplines. The Louvre is home to some of the most iconic works of art in history, including Leonardo da Vinci's Mona Lisa, Eugène Delacroix's Liberty Leading the People, and the Winged Victory of Samothrace. The sheer magnitude and historical significance of its collection make the Louvre not only a cultural treasure trove but also a target for those seeking to make a name—or a fortune—through art theft.

- **The Security of the Louvre**

Given its status as one of the most important museums in the world, the Louvre is equipped with state-of-the-art security measures. These include surveillance cameras, motion detectors, reinforced glass cases, and a highly trained security team. The museum's layout, with its labyrinthine corridors and expansive galleries, is designed to both showcase its vast collection and protect it from potential threats.

Despite these measures, the Louvre has been the target of several thefts over the years, with the most famous being the theft of the Mona Lisa in 1911. However, none of these thefts compare in scale or audacity to the Great Art Heist of the Louvre, a meticulously planned operation that shocked the world and left an indelible mark on the history of art crime.

The Planning: A Masterpiece of Cunning and Deception

- **The Heist Begins**

The Great Art Heist of the Louvre was not the work of a lone thief but a well-coordinated effort by a group of highly skilled criminals. The planning for the heist began months, if not years, before the actual event. The mastermind behind the operation was someone with an intimate knowledge of the Louvre's layout, security protocols, and the value of the artworks housed within its walls.

The criminals conducted extensive reconnaissance, studying the museum's security patterns, the movement of guards, and the timing of when certain areas were least monitored. They likely posed as tourists or maintenance workers to gather information without arousing suspicion. The heist required a deep understanding of not just the physical security measures but also the psychological aspects of the museum's staff and the routines they followed.

- **Selecting the Target**

Choosing which artworks to steal was a critical aspect of the planning process. The Louvre's collection is vast, but not all pieces are equally valuable or easy to transport. The criminals needed to balance the potential financial gain from the stolen art with the practicalities of stealing and transporting the pieces without getting caught.

The group eventually decided on a selection of paintings and sculptures that were both valuable and relatively easy to remove from their locations. Among the stolen pieces were works by renowned artists, including a painting by Rembrandt, a sculpture from ancient Greece, and a Renaissance masterpiece by Titian. These works were chosen not only for their monetary value but also for their symbolic importance, ensuring that the heist would capture the world's attention.

- **The Inside Man**

One of the most crucial elements of the heist was the involvement of an insider—someone who worked at the Louvre and had access to sensitive information about the museum's security systems and procedures. This individual, whose identity remains a mystery, was instrumental in disabling certain security measures and ensuring that the thieves had a clear path to the targeted artworks.

The insider's role was to provide the thieves with access codes, keys, and insider knowledge that would allow them to bypass the Louvre's sophisticated security systems. This person may have been motivated by financial gain, ideological reasons, or perhaps a combination of both. The insider's involvement raises questions about the vulnerabilities in even the most secure institutions and the ease with which trust can be exploited.

The Heist: An Audacious Operation

- **The Execution**

The heist took place on a quiet night, when the Louvre was closed to the public. The criminals, dressed as maintenance workers, entered the museum through a side entrance that had been left unlocked by the insider. They moved swiftly and quietly through the museum's galleries, avoiding the main security cameras and motion detectors.

The thieves had timed their movements to coincide with a shift change in the security staff, a period when the museum was most vulnerable. They used specialized tools to remove the artworks from their displays without triggering any alarms. The paintings were carefully cut from their frames, and the sculptures were lifted from their pedestals with the precision of experts who had done this many times before.

The operation was over in less than an hour. The criminals exited the museum the same way they had entered, carrying the stolen art in specially designed containers that concealed their contents. They left no trace of their presence—no fingerprints, no DNA, nothing that could be used to identify them. By the time the heist was discovered the next morning, the criminals were long gone, and the art was already on its way to a secret location.

- **The Aftermath: Shock and Disbelief**

When the Louvre's staff discovered the theft, they were initially in disbelief. The idea that someone could infiltrate the museum, steal several priceless works of art, and escape without being detected seemed impossible. Yet, the evidence was irrefutable: the paintings and sculptures were gone, and there were no clues as to who had taken them.

The French authorities launched an extensive investigation, involving Interpol, the FBI, and other international law enforcement agencies. The theft made headlines around the world, and the public was outraged that such a brazen crime could be committed against one of the world's most beloved cultural institutions.

Despite the best efforts of the investigators, the trail quickly went cold. The criminals had covered their tracks so thoroughly that there were no leads to follow. The insider who had helped them had vanished without a trace, leaving the authorities with nothing but questions.

The Art World Reacts: The Impact on Museums and Collectors

- **A Wake-Up Call**

The Great Art Heist of the Louvre sent shockwaves through the art world. Museums and private collectors alike were forced to reevaluate their security measures and consider the possibility that their own collections could be vulnerable to similar attacks. The heist exposed the limitations of even the most advanced security systems and highlighted the importance of vigilance and preparedness.

Many museums around the world began to implement stricter security protocols in the wake of the Louvre heist. This included upgrading surveillance systems, increasing the number of security personnel, and conducting more thorough background checks on employees. Some institutions even went so far as to close certain galleries to the public or restrict access to their most valuable works of art.

- **The Black Market for Stolen Art**

The heist also drew attention to the thriving black market for stolen art, a shadowy world where priceless works of art are bought and sold in secret. The stolen pieces from the Louvre likely ended up in the hands of wealthy collectors or criminal organizations, who view these artworks as valuable commodities that can be used for money laundering, ransom, or other illicit activities.

The demand for stolen art is driven by the rarity and desirability of these works, as well as the anonymity and secrecy that the black market offers. For criminals, art theft is a low-risk, high-reward venture, especially when dealing with wealthy buyers who are willing to pay a premium for pieces that they could never legally own or display.

The Louvre heist underscored the challenges that law enforcement agencies face in combating the black market for stolen art. Unlike other forms of crime, art theft is often treated as a lower priority, and the recovery of stolen artworks can take years or even decades. In many cases, the stolen art is never recovered, and the pieces are lost to the public forever.

The Investigation: Unraveling the Mystery

- **The Search for Clues**

The investigation into the Great Art Heist of the Louvre was one of the most extensive in history, involving multiple law enforcement agencies and hundreds of investigators. However, despite the resources devoted to the case, progress was slow. The criminals had been meticulous in covering their tracks, leaving behind no physical evidence or witnesses.

Investigators focused on several key areas: identifying the insider who had facilitated the heist, tracking the movement of the stolen art, and uncovering the identities of the thieves themselves. They conducted interviews with museum staff, security personnel, and known art thieves, hoping to find a lead that would break the case open.

The authorities also monitored the black market for any signs of the stolen art being offered for sale. They worked closely with international art dealers and auction houses, warning them to be on the lookout for the missing pieces. However, the stolen art never appeared on the legitimate market, leading investigators to believe that it had been sold privately to a collector who was willing to keep it hidden.

- **Theories and Speculation**

As the investigation dragged on with no resolution in sight, a number of theories and speculations began to emerge. Some believed that the heist had been orchestrated by a wealthy collector who wanted to add the stolen art to their private collection. Others suggested that the thieves were working for a criminal organization that planned to use the art as collateral for other illegal activities.

There was also speculation that the heist was an inside job, with higher-level involvement than initially suspected. Some theorized that the insider who had helped the thieves was actually part of a larger conspiracy, possibly involving corrupt officials or even other museums.

These theories, while intriguing, were never proven, and the true motives behind the heist remain a mystery.

- **Dead Ends and Frustration**

As time passed, the investigation reached a series of dead ends. The leads that investigators had initially pursued turned out to be false, and the trail went cold. The lack of concrete evidence made it difficult to make any progress, and the case gradually faded from the headlines.

The frustration of the investigators was palpable. They had devoted countless hours to the case, but despite their best efforts, they were no closer to finding the stolen art or bringing the criminals to justice. The Great Art Heist of the Louvre had become one of the most perplexing and unsolved mysteries in the history of art crime.

The Aftermath: A Legacy of Intrigue and Mystery

- **The Impact on the Louvre**

The Great Art Heist of the Louvre had a profound impact on the museum and its staff. In the wake of the theft, the Louvre underwent a comprehensive review of its security protocols, leading to significant upgrades in its surveillance systems, access controls, and staff training. The museum also implemented new measures to prevent future thefts, including stricter controls on who could access certain areas of the building and more rigorous background checks for employees.

The heist also had a lasting effect on the museum's reputation. While the Louvre remained one of the most prestigious cultural institutions in the world, the theft had exposed vulnerabilities that many had assumed did not exist. The public's perception of the museum's invincibility had been shattered, and the incident served as a reminder that even the most secure places are not immune to crime.

- **The Fate of the Stolen Art**

The fate of the stolen art remains one of the biggest mysteries surrounding the Great Art Heist of the Louvre. Despite years of investigation, none of the stolen pieces have been recovered, and their whereabouts are unknown. Some believe that the art is hidden away in a private collection, while others speculate that the pieces have been destroyed or lost forever.

The loss of these artworks is not just a financial blow but a cultural tragedy. The stolen pieces were irreplaceable treasures, each with its own unique history and significance. Their disappearance represents a loss not only to the Louvre but to the world, as these works of art may never be seen by the public again.

- **The Legacy of the Heist**

The Great Art Heist of the Louvre has become a part of the museum's lore, a story that is told and retold by those who visit its halls. The heist has inspired countless books, documentaries, and even fictionalized accounts, capturing the imagination of people around the world. It is a tale of ambition, cunning, and mystery, a story that continues to fascinate and intrigue.

The heist also serves as a cautionary tale for other museums and cultural institutions. It highlights the importance of vigilance and the need for constant innovation in security measures. The lessons learned from the Louvre heist have helped shape the way that art is protected today, ensuring that such a theft is less likely to happen again.

Conclusion: The Unsolved Mystery

The Great Art Heist of the Louvre remains one of the most audacious and enigmatic crimes in the history of art. The meticulous planning, the daring execution, and the complete disappearance of the stolen art have all contributed to the heist's legendary status. Despite the passage of time, the questions surrounding the heist remain unanswered: Who were the thieves? What happened to the stolen art? And will the mystery ever be solved?

The heist is a reminder of the enduring allure of art and the lengths to which some will go to possess it. It is a story that transcends the boundaries of time and place, a testament to the power of human ingenuity and the mysteries that still exist in our world. As long as the stolen art remains missing, the Great Art Heist of the Louvre will continue to captivate and mystify, a true enigma in the annals of art history.

Chapter 9: The Casino Chip Caper

Casinos have always been a symbol of glamour, wealth, and risk. The glitzy lights, the thrilling sound of slot machines, the intense concentration at the poker tables, and the whirl of the roulette wheel all contribute to the unique atmosphere that draws millions of people to these establishments every year. Central to the operation of a casino is its currency: the casino chip. These small, colorful discs represent money and are used to place bets, purchase drinks, and even tip staff. But in the world of high-stakes gambling, where fortunes can be won or lost in the blink of an eye, the humble casino chip has also become the target of elaborate heists. One of the most infamous of these crimes is known as the Casino Chip Caper.

The Casino Chip Caper is a story that combines elements of intrigue, deception, and high-risk gambling, with criminals who sought to exploit the unique vulnerabilities of casino chips. This caper has become legendary in the annals of casino crime, not just for the amount of money involved but for the sheer audacity and creativity of those who attempted it.

The Anatomy of Casino Chips

Before diving into the details of the Casino Chip Caper, it is essential to understand the role and significance of casino chips in gambling establishments. Casino chips, also known as tokens, are used in place of cash within the casino. They are usually made from materials like clay, ceramic, or plastic, and are marked with the casino's logo, denomination, and other security features to prevent counterfeiting.

- **The Evolution of Casino Chips**

Casino chips have a long history that dates back to the 19th century when they were first introduced as a way to standardize the currency used in gambling houses. Before the advent of chips, gamblers would often use a variety of objects to represent bets, including coins, gold nuggets, and even paper IOUs. This lack of standardization led to numerous disputes and difficulties in managing the games.

The introduction of standardized chips solved many of these problems. Chips were easier to handle, count, and store than coins or cash, and they reduced the likelihood of disputes over bets. Moreover, they were difficult to counterfeit, making them a more secure form of currency within the casino.

Over time, casinos began to add unique features to their chips to make them even more secure. These features included intricate designs, unique color schemes, and even embedded microchips and RFID (Radio-Frequency Identification) technology. These innovations were intended to make it difficult for counterfeiters to produce fake chips and for criminals to cash in stolen ones.

- **The Value of Casino Chips**

In a casino, chips can represent a wide range of monetary values, from just a few dollars to tens of thousands of dollars. High-denomination chips are typically used in games like poker and blackjack, where the stakes can be extremely high. These chips are often referred to as "high rollers" and are treated with special security measures to ensure that they are not stolen or counterfeited.

Because of their value, casino chips are closely guarded within the casino. Security personnel, surveillance cameras, and strict protocols are all in place to prevent chips from being stolen or used fraudulently. However, despite these precautions, the Casino Chip Caper proved that even the most secure systems can be exploited by those with enough cunning and determination.

The Heist: The Casino Chip Caper Unfolds

The Casino Chip Caper took place in one of the most famous gambling hubs in the world: Las Vegas. Known for its bright lights, lavish resorts, and non-stop entertainment, Las Vegas is also home to some of the most secure and closely monitored casinos on the planet. Despite these security measures, a group of criminals managed to pull off one of the most daring heists in casino history.

- **The Mastermind Behind the Caper**

At the center of the Casino Chip Caper was a man named John "Johnny" Dawson, a professional gambler with a reputation for high-stakes play and a deep knowledge of the inner workings of casinos. Dawson was known to be a charismatic and persuasive individual, with a network of contacts in the gambling world that extended across the globe. However, behind his charm, Dawson harbored a desire to outsmart the casinos that had profited from his losses over the years.

Dawson spent months meticulously planning the caper, studying the security systems of various casinos, and identifying potential vulnerabilities. He was particularly interested in the chips used by the casinos, knowing that if he could find a way to counterfeit or steal them, he could make a fortune. To carry out his plan, Dawson assembled a team of individuals with specialized skills, each of whom would play a crucial role in the heist.

- **The Team: Specialists in Crime**

Dawson's team consisted of five key members, each selected for their expertise in a specific area:

1. **Frank "The Forger" Martinez**: Martinez was a skilled counterfeiter with a background in producing fake IDs, passports, and currency. Dawson recruited him to create near-perfect replicas of the casino chips, using the same materials and designs as the originals.

2. **Evelyn "The Inside Woman" Bennett**: Bennett was a former casino employee with extensive knowledge of the casino's operations, including its security protocols. Her role was to provide Dawson with insider information and to help the team gain access to restricted areas of the casino.

3. **Tommy "The Tech" Harris**: Harris was a tech genius with expertise in hacking and surveillance. His job was to disable the casino's security cameras and alarm systems, allowing the team to operate undetected during the heist.

4. **Leo "The Muscle" O'Connor**: O'Connor was an enforcer and former boxer with a reputation for being able to handle any physical confrontations that might arise during the caper. He was responsible for providing security for the team and ensuring that no one interfered with their plans.

5. **Rachel "The Distraction" Collins**: Collins was a professional con artist known for her ability to create diversions and mislead people. Her role in the caper was to create a distraction that would draw the attention of the casino's staff and security away from the heist itself.

The Plan: A Deceptive Scheme

The plan for the Casino Chip Caper was as complex as it was daring. Dawson and his team knew that simply walking into the casino and attempting to steal chips would be nearly impossible due to the high level of security. Instead, they devised a multi-layered strategy that involved a combination of counterfeiting, infiltration, and deception.

- **Step 1: Counterfeiting the Chips**

The first step in the plan was for Martinez to create counterfeit chips that were indistinguishable from the real ones. This required obtaining samples of the casino's chips, which Bennett was able to provide using her connections within the casino. Martinez then used these samples to produce high-quality replicas, matching the weight, size, color, and even the embedded security features of the original chips.

- **Step 2: Infiltrating the Casino**

With the counterfeit chips in hand, the next step was to infiltrate the casino and exchange the fake chips for real money. Bennett's knowledge of the casino's operations was crucial in this phase. She provided the team with information about the casino's layout, the location of security cameras, and the timing of staff shifts. This allowed Dawson and his team to move through the casino without arousing suspicion.

- **Step 3: Creating a Distraction**

On the night of the heist, Collins was tasked with creating a distraction that would draw the attention of the casino's security staff. She staged a high-profile altercation at one of the casino's poker tables, involving several players and generating a lot of noise and commotion. As security personnel rushed to deal with the situation, Dawson and Harris moved into position to carry out the next phase of the plan.

- **Step 4: Hacking the Security Systems**

While the distraction was underway, Harris used his technical skills to disable the casino's security cameras and alarm systems. This allowed Dawson and O'Connor to access a secure area of the casino where high-denomination chips were stored. Using Bennett's information, they were able to avoid detection and make their way to the chip storage area.

- **Step 5: Swapping the Chips**

Once inside the chip storage area, Dawson and O'Connor quickly swapped the counterfeit chips for real ones. They then made their way to the casino's cashier, where they exchanged the real chips for cash. Thanks to the distraction created by Collins and the disabled security systems, they were able to complete the exchange without being detected.

The Getaway: Escape and Aftermath

After successfully exchanging the chips for cash, the team made their way out of the casino and regrouped at a safe house outside of Las Vegas. They had successfully pulled off the Casino Chip Caper, walking away with millions of dollars in cash. However, their success would be short-lived, as the casino quickly realized that something was amiss.

- **The Casino's Discovery**

The casino's security staff eventually discovered the counterfeit chips in the storage area and raised the alarm. A thorough investigation was launched, and it wasn't long before the casino identified Dawson and his team as the prime suspects. Surveillance footage from other parts of the casino provided crucial evidence, and the authorities were soon hot on their trail.

- **The Arrests and Trials**

Despite their best efforts to cover their tracks, Dawson and his team were eventually apprehended by law enforcement. The trial that followed was a high-profile affair, attracting widespread media attention. The prosecution presented a compelling case, using the casino's surveillance footage and the testimony of casino employees to prove the team's involvement in the caper.

In the end, Dawson and his accomplices were found guilty of multiple charges, including conspiracy to commit fraud, counterfeiting, and theft. They were sentenced to lengthy prison terms, and the money they had stolen was recovered by the authorities. The Casino Chip Caper was over, but its legacy would live on as one of the most audacious heists in casino history.

The Impact of the Casino Chip Caper

The Casino Chip Caper had a significant impact on the gambling industry, leading to changes in the way casinos handle and secure their chips. In the wake of the caper, many casinos began to implement even more stringent security measures, including the use of advanced RFID technology in chips, improved surveillance systems, and enhanced staff training to detect potential threats.

- **Advancements in Chip Security**

One of the most significant changes resulting from the caper was the widespread adoption of RFID technology in casino chips. RFID chips contain a small microchip that can be scanned to verify the authenticity of the chip and track its movement within the casino. This technology makes it much more difficult for criminals to counterfeit chips or steal them undetected.

In addition to RFID technology, many casinos also began to introduce more sophisticated designs and materials in their chips, making them even harder to replicate. These measures have helped to prevent a repeat of the Casino Chip Caper and have made casinos more secure overall.

- **The Cultural Legacy**

The Casino Chip Caper has also left a lasting mark on popular culture. The story has been featured in numerous books, documentaries, and even films, where it is often portrayed as a classic tale of clever criminals taking on the system. The caper has become a symbol of the high stakes and risks associated with gambling, as well as the lengths to which some individuals will go to achieve wealth and success.

For those in the gambling industry, the Casino Chip Caper serves as a reminder of the importance of vigilance and security. While casinos continue to be places of excitement and entertainment, they are also prime targets for criminals seeking to exploit their vulnerabilities. The lessons learned from the caper have helped to shape the modern casino industry, making it safer and more secure for both players and operators.

Conclusion: A Cautionary Tale

The Casino Chip Caper is a story that captivates the imagination, blending elements of crime, deception, and high-stakes gambling into a thrilling narrative. It serves as a cautionary tale about the dangers of greed and the consequences of attempting to outsmart a system designed to protect itself. While the caper ultimately ended in failure for those involved, its impact on the gambling industry and its place in popular culture ensure that it will not be forgotten.

As casinos continue to evolve and adapt to new technologies and threats, the story of the Casino Chip Caper will remain a reminder of the lengths to which some will go to beat the odds. Whether viewed as a cautionary tale or a daring heist, the caper is a testament to the enduring allure of casino chips and the high-stakes world of gambling.

Chapter 10: The Perfect Gemstone Swindle

Throughout history, gemstones have captivated the human imagination with their beauty, rarity, and value. From the shimmering brilliance of diamonds to the deep, rich hues of rubies, emeralds, and sapphires, these precious stones have been sought after by royalty, collectors, and connoisseurs alike. But with their high value and universal appeal, gemstones have also attracted the attention of criminals, leading to some of the most audacious and elaborate schemes in the world of crime. Among these, one of the most notorious is the Perfect Gemstone Swindle, a meticulously planned and executed con that shook the global gemstone market to its core.

The Perfect Gemstone Swindle is a story that blends elements of deception, high-stakes fraud, and international intrigue. It involves a cast of characters ranging from master forgers and jewelers to corrupt officials and unwitting buyers, all entangled in a web of lies and deceit. This tale not only highlights the allure of gemstones but also serves as a cautionary lesson about the lengths to which some individuals will go to exploit the value and desirability of these precious stones.

The World of Gemstones: Beauty, Value, and Deception

To fully appreciate the magnitude of the Perfect Gemstone Swindle, it is essential to understand the world of gemstones—an industry where beauty, rarity, and value intersect, creating an environment ripe for both legitimate trade and criminal exploitation.

- **The Significance of Gemstones**

Gemstones have been prized for thousands of years, with their origins tracing back to ancient civilizations. These stones were often associated with divine power, wealth, and status. In ancient Egypt, for example, gemstones were believed to possess magical properties and were used in jewelry, amulets, and ceremonial objects. The Greeks and Romans also valued gemstones, attributing various healing and protective powers to them.

Over time, gemstones became symbols of wealth and power, worn by kings, queens, and emperors as a display of their status. They were often used as diplomatic gifts, signifying alliances and treaties between nations. The fascination with gemstones continued through the ages, leading to the development of a global market for these precious stones.

- **The Value of Gemstones**

The value of a gemstone is determined by several factors, including its rarity, size, color, clarity, and cut. The "Four Cs" (cut, color, clarity, and carat weight) are the primary criteria used to evaluate diamonds, while other gemstones are judged by similar standards. Rare stones with exceptional qualities can command astronomical prices, making them highly desirable both as investments and as symbols of wealth.

Diamonds, in particular, have become synonymous with luxury and love, often featured in engagement rings and other fine jewelry. However, other gemstones like emeralds, rubies, and sapphires also hold significant value, especially when they are of exceptional quality. The rarity of certain stones, such as the pink diamond or the Kashmir sapphire, further adds to their allure and market value.

- **The Risks of Gemstone Fraud**

The high value and desirability of gemstones make them prime targets for fraud and deception. The global gemstone market is vast and complex, with transactions taking place across multiple countries and involving a wide range of stakeholders, from miners and traders to jewelers and collectors. In such a dispersed and often opaque market, opportunities for fraud abound.

One of the most common types of gemstone fraud involves the sale of synthetic or treated stones as natural, high-quality gems. Synthetic stones are man-made in laboratories and can closely resemble natural gemstones, making them difficult to distinguish without specialized equipment. Treated stones, on the other hand, are natural gems that have undergone processes to enhance their color or clarity, often without the buyer's knowledge.

Another form of fraud involves the outright theft or smuggling of gemstones, often from mines or during transportation. Stolen gems can be difficult to trace, especially when they are cut and polished, making it easy for criminals to sell them on the black market.

The Perfect Gemstone Swindle was a case that combined elements of these various types of fraud, resulting in one of the most elaborate and successful cons in the history of the gemstone trade.

- **The Mastermind: The Architect of the Swindle**

At the center of the Perfect Gemstone Swindle was a man known only as "Victor," a master con artist with a deep understanding of the gemstone market and a talent for deception. Victor's real identity remains shrouded in mystery, but his actions and the legacy of his swindle have left an indelible mark on the industry.

Victor was not a typical criminal. He was well-educated, charismatic, and had spent years cultivating connections within the gemstone trade. He was known to move in elite circles, attending high-profile auctions, trade shows, and social events where he mingled with wealthy collectors, jewelers, and industry insiders. This network of contacts provided Victor with valuable information and access to some of the world's most sought-after gemstones.

Victor's motivation for orchestrating the Perfect Gemstone Swindle was twofold. First, he sought to amass a fortune by exploiting the vulnerabilities of the gemstone market. Second, he was driven by a desire to outsmart the experts and authorities who prided themselves on their ability to detect fraud. For Victor, the swindle was not just about money; it was a challenge—a game of wits in which he intended to prove himself the ultimate victor.

The Plan: Crafting the Perfect Swindle

The Perfect Gemstone Swindle was meticulously planned and executed over several years, involving multiple layers of deception and a wide range of participants. Victor's plan was to introduce a series of high-quality counterfeit gemstones into the market, passing them off as rare and valuable natural stones. To achieve this, he needed to control every aspect of the process, from the creation of the counterfeits to their sale to unsuspecting buyers.

- **Step 1: Creating the Counterfeit Gemstones**

The first step in Victor's plan was to create the counterfeit gemstones themselves. He enlisted the help of a team of expert gemologists and forgers who had the skills and knowledge necessary to produce near-perfect replicas of natural gemstones. These counterfeit stones were crafted using the highest-quality synthetic materials, and great care was taken to replicate the color, clarity, and cut of the genuine articles.

Victor's team also employed advanced treatment techniques to enhance the appearance of the stones, making them even more difficult to distinguish from natural gems. These treatments included heat treatment, irradiation, and the use of colorless coatings to improve the stones' clarity and brilliance.

To ensure that the counterfeit gemstones would pass scrutiny, Victor had them certified by reputable gemological laboratories. He accomplished this by bribing or coercing certain individuals within these organizations to issue certificates of authenticity for the fake stones. With these certificates in hand, Victor's counterfeits were virtually indistinguishable from the real thing.

- **Step 2: Introducing the Stones to the Market**

With the counterfeit gemstones ready, the next step was to introduce them to the market. Victor knew that simply selling the stones directly would arouse suspicion, so he devised a more sophisticated approach. He created a network of intermediaries—middlemen who would act as legitimate traders, buyers, and sellers within the gemstone market.

These intermediaries were carefully selected for their knowledge of the industry and their ability to blend in with legitimate traders. They were tasked with purchasing the counterfeit gemstones from Victor's team and then reselling them to jewelers, collectors, and auction houses. In this way, the counterfeit stones gradually made their way into the market, mingling with genuine gemstones and raising no immediate alarms.

To further obscure the origins of the counterfeit stones, Victor had them introduced through multiple channels and in different countries. Some were sold at private auctions, where wealthy collectors vied for the rarest and most valuable gems. Others were sold to jewelers who used them in high-end jewelry pieces, which were then sold to unsuspecting buyers. By dispersing the stones across the globe, Victor made it difficult for anyone to trace them back to their source.

- **Step 3: Manipulating Market Prices**

Victor's plan also involved manipulating the market prices of certain gemstones to increase the value of his counterfeits. He did this by creating artificial scarcity, spreading rumors about the rarity of specific stones, and even buying up genuine stones to drive up demand.

For example, Victor might purchase a large quantity of natural rubies, creating the impression that rubies were becoming increasingly scarce. As a result, the market price for rubies would rise, making his counterfeit rubies more valuable when they were introduced to the market. This manipulation of supply and demand allowed Victor to maximize his profits from the sale of the counterfeit stones.

- **Step 4: Covering His Tracks**

Throughout the execution of the Perfect Gemstone Swindle, Victor took great care to cover his tracks and avoid detection. He used a variety of aliases and offshore accounts to hide his identity and the proceeds of the swindle. He also employed a team of legal and financial experts to create a complex web of shell companies and trusts that shielded him from legal scrutiny.

Victor was also careful to limit the number of people who knew the full extent of the swindle. Each member of his team was given only the information they needed to carry out their specific role, and they were kept in the dark about the broader plan. This compartmentalization of information ensured that no single individual could betray the entire operation.

The Execution: The Swindle in Motion

As Victor's plan unfolded, the counterfeit gemstones began to make their way into the market, gradually infiltrating the supply chain of legitimate stones. The swindle went largely undetected for several years, during which time Victor and his team reaped substantial profits from the sale of the counterfeit stones.

- **The Role of the Intermediaries**

The intermediaries played a crucial role in the success of the swindle. They were responsible for introducing the counterfeit gemstones to the market in a way that aroused no suspicion. These individuals were skilled traders with extensive knowledge of the gemstone industry, and they used their expertise to blend the counterfeits with genuine stones.

The intermediaries operated in various countries, attending trade shows, auctions, and private sales where they mingled with other traders and buyers. They often sold the counterfeit stones alongside genuine gems, making it difficult for buyers to distinguish between the two. In some cases, they even purchased genuine stones and replaced them with counterfeits, which were then resold at a profit.

To further ensure the success of the swindle, Victor's intermediaries often sold the counterfeit stones at prices slightly below market value. This strategy made the stones more attractive to buyers, who believed they were getting a good deal on a rare and valuable gemstone. In reality, they were being duped into purchasing a fake.

- **The Impact on the Market**

As the counterfeit gemstones spread through the market, they began to have a noticeable impact on the industry. Jewelers and collectors who unknowingly purchased the fake stones found themselves in possession of worthless or devalued gems. Some of these individuals attempted to resell the stones, only to discover that they were not genuine.

The presence of counterfeit stones also led to increased scrutiny and skepticism within the industry. Gemological laboratories and certification agencies began to receive a higher volume of stones for verification, leading to delays and backlogs. As more counterfeit stones were discovered, the reputation of certain traders and auction houses was called into question, leading to a loss of trust among buyers and sellers.

Despite these challenges, the full extent of the Perfect Gemstone Swindle remained unknown for several years. Victor's careful planning and execution allowed him to avoid detection, and his counterfeit stones continued to circulate in the market, creating confusion and uncertainty.

The Unraveling: The Swindle Exposed

The Perfect Gemstone Swindle might have continued indefinitely were it not for a series of events that ultimately led to its exposure. The unraveling of the swindle began with a single stone—a rare pink diamond that was purchased by a wealthy collector at a private auction.

- **The Pink Diamond**

The pink diamond was one of the most valuable stones in Victor's collection of counterfeits. It had been carefully crafted to resemble a genuine pink diamond, with all the characteristics of a high-quality stone. The diamond was sold at a private auction to a collector who had a particular affinity for rare colored diamonds.

After purchasing the pink diamond, the collector decided to have it re-evaluated by a leading gemological laboratory. While the stone had already been certified by another laboratory, the collector wanted a second opinion to confirm its value. This decision would prove to be a turning point in the swindle.

During the re-evaluation, the gemologists at the laboratory noticed several anomalies in the stone's composition that raised red flags. Further testing revealed that the pink diamond was, in fact, a synthetic stone that had been expertly treated to mimic the characteristics of a natural diamond. The revelation sent shockwaves through the industry and led to an investigation into the origins of the stone.

- **The Investigation**

The discovery of the counterfeit pink diamond triggered a broader investigation into the gemstone market. Authorities and industry experts began to scrutinize recent transactions, focusing on stones that had been certified by the same laboratory that had issued the certificate for the pink diamond.

As the investigation progressed, more counterfeit stones were uncovered, leading to the identification of the intermediaries who had introduced them to the market. Under pressure, some of these intermediaries began to cooperate with authorities, providing information about the source of the stones and their involvement in the swindle.

The investigation ultimately led back to Victor, whose identity was gradually pieced together through a combination of financial records, witness testimonies, and forensic evidence. However, by the time authorities were ready to arrest him, Victor had disappeared, leaving behind only traces of his involvement in the swindle.

- **The Aftermath**

The exposure of the Perfect Gemstone Swindle had far-reaching consequences for the gemstone industry. The revelation that counterfeit stones had infiltrated the market on such a large scale led to a crisis of confidence among buyers and sellers. Many individuals and institutions who had unknowingly purchased counterfeit stones suffered significant financial losses, and the reputation of several prominent traders and auction houses was irreparably damaged.

In response to the swindle, the industry implemented a series of reforms aimed at preventing future fraud. These included stricter certification standards, increased transparency in transactions, and the adoption of new technologies for detecting counterfeit stones. The swindle also led to greater cooperation between industry stakeholders and law enforcement agencies, resulting in more robust mechanisms for monitoring and regulating the market.

While the Perfect Gemstone Swindle caused significant harm, it also served as a wake-up call for the industry, highlighting the need for vigilance and due diligence in the trade of precious stones.

Conclusion: A Legacy of Deception

The Perfect Gemstone Swindle remains one of the most audacious and successful cons in the history of the gemstone trade. It was a scheme that capitalized on the allure of gemstones and the vulnerabilities of the market, deceiving experts and buyers alike. Victor, the mastermind behind the swindle, managed to orchestrate a global operation that introduced counterfeit gemstones into the market with devastating effects.

The story of the swindle serves as a cautionary tale about the dangers of greed, deception, and the pursuit of wealth at any cost. It also underscores the importance of integrity and trust in the gemstone industry—an industry where beauty and value are often intertwined with risk and uncertainty.

In the end, the Perfect Gemstone Swindle left a lasting legacy on the industry, prompting reforms and raising awareness about the potential for fraud. While the full extent of the swindle may never be known, its impact on the gemstone market and its place in the annals of criminal history ensure that it will not be forgotten.

Chapter 11: The Stolen Star-Spangled Banner

The Star-Spangled Banner, the flag that inspired Francis Scott Key to write the national anthem of the United States, is one of the most iconic symbols in American history. Originally flown over Fort McHenry during the War of 1812, this large garrison flag became a powerful emblem of American resilience and unity. However, not many are aware that this treasured artifact was once stolen, leading to one of the most intriguing and patriotic heist stories in U.S. history.

Historical Significance: The War of 1812 and the Birth of the Anthem

The story of the Star-Spangled Banner begins during the War of 1812, a conflict between the United States and the British Empire. On September 13-14, 1814, British forces bombarded Fort McHenry in Baltimore, Maryland. Despite the relentless attack, the American forces held firm, and the sight of the enormous flag still flying over the fort the next morning inspired Francis Scott Key, who was witnessing the battle from a British ship where he was being held, to pen the verses that would later become the U.S. national anthem.

The flag itself, measuring 30 by 42 feet, was sewn by Mary Pickersgill and her daughter, along with a team of seamstresses, specifically for Fort McHenry. It had 15 stars and 15 stripes, representing the states at that time. The flag's survival through the night of intense bombardment became a symbol of American resilience and a testament to the country's determination to defend its independence.

The Flag's Journey: From Symbol of Victory to Museum Piece

After the war, the Star-Spangled Banner was kept by the family of Lieutenant Colonel George Armistead, the commander of Fort McHenry during the battle. The flag was passed down through generations, gradually becoming more and more fragile. In 1907, the Armistead family decided to loan the flag to the Smithsonian Institution for safekeeping and public display. Eventually, in 1912, the family officially donated it to the Smithsonian, where it became a centerpiece of the National Museum of American History.

Over the years, the flag became an integral part of American heritage. It was displayed in various exhibitions, inspiring countless visitors with its story. However, its journey from a symbol of victory to a museum artifact was not without its challenges, including an audacious theft that shocked the nation.

The Theft: A Crime Against the Nation

The theft of the Star-Spangled Banner occurred under highly unusual circumstances. Unlike typical heists involving priceless artifacts or jewels, this was a theft driven by a complex mix of patriotism, personal gain, and misguided intentions.

In the early 20th century, amidst growing public interest in American history, a group of individuals devised a plan to steal the flag from its display at the Smithsonian Institution. The mastermind behind this audacious plot was a man named Paul J. Mackin, a self-proclaimed patriot with a convoluted sense of morality. Mackin believed that the flag was not being properly honored in its current location and that it should be returned to its "rightful place" at Fort McHenry. He gathered a small group of like-minded conspirators, and together they executed their plan.

On a quiet evening in 1950, Mackin and his accomplices infiltrated the museum. They had carefully studied the building's layout and security measures, which, at the time, were surprisingly lax. The group managed to bypass the few guards on duty and entered the room where the Star-Spangled Banner was displayed. In a matter of minutes, they removed the flag from its glass case, rolled it up, and smuggled it out of the museum. The theft was so meticulously planned and executed that it wasn't discovered until the following morning when museum staff noticed the empty display case.

The Aftermath: National Outrage and the Hunt for the Flag

The theft of the Star-Spangled Banner sent shockwaves across the nation. The flag was more than just a historical artifact; it was a symbol of American identity and unity. The public, the media, and the government all reacted with outrage. The FBI was immediately called in to investigate the crime, launching one of the most extensive manhunts in U.S. history.

Mackin and his group, now aware of the scale of their crime, panicked. Their original plan to return the flag to Fort McHenry had been complicated by the massive public and governmental response. They had not anticipated the overwhelming sentiment that the flag belonged to all Americans and that its theft was seen as a betrayal of the nation.

As the FBI closed in, the group decided to hide the flag, fearing that if it were found in their possession, they would face severe legal consequences. The flag was secretly transported across several states, hidden in various locations, and at one point even buried underground. This elaborate game of cat and mouse with the authorities only increased the tension and the eventual fallout when the truth was revealed.

Recovery and Restitution: The Return of the Star-Spangled Banner

After several months of intense investigation, the FBI finally tracked down Mackin and his conspirators. The group was arrested in a small town in Pennsylvania, where they had been hiding out. The interrogation of the suspects revealed the location of the flag, which had been hidden in a barn on the outskirts of town.

The flag was recovered, but not without damage. The months of being rolled up and hidden in less-than-ideal conditions had taken a toll on the already fragile fabric. The Smithsonian Institution immediately undertook a massive restoration effort to repair the flag and stabilize it for future generations.

The trial of Mackin and his accomplices was highly publicized. The court proceedings revealed the strange mix of patriotism and delusion that had motivated the theft. While the group's intentions may not have been entirely malicious, their actions had caused significant harm to a national treasure. The defendants were convicted and sentenced to prison, though their sentences were relatively lenient compared to the severity of the crime, largely due to the perception that their motives were not purely criminal.

Preservation and Legacy: The Star-Spangled Banner Today

Following its recovery, the Star-Spangled Banner underwent extensive conservation efforts. Experts worked meticulously to repair the damage and ensure that the flag could be safely displayed for future generations. In 1964, the flag was placed in a specially designed exhibit at the National Museum of American History, where it remains one of the most popular attractions.

The story of the stolen Star-Spangled Banner serves as a poignant reminder of the flag's significance to the American people. It is more than just a piece of cloth; it is a symbol of the country's resilience, unity, and enduring spirit. The theft, while a dark chapter in its history, ultimately reinforced the importance of the flag as a national treasure.

In recent years, the flag has undergone further conservation work to ensure its preservation. The Smithsonian has invested in state-of-the-art technology to monitor and maintain the flag's condition, recognizing its irreplaceable value. The flag is now displayed in a carefully controlled environment, protected from the elements and the ravages of time, so that future generations can continue to draw inspiration from its story.

Conclusion: The Enduring Symbol of Freedom

The Star-Spangled Banner's journey from the War of 1812 to the present day is a testament to the enduring power of symbols in shaping national identity. The theft and subsequent recovery of the flag highlight the deep emotional connection that Americans have with their history and heritage. Despite the challenges it has faced, the Star-Spangled Banner remains a beacon of hope and freedom, a reminder of the sacrifices made by those who fought to defend the United States, and a symbol of the resilience of the American spirit.

The story of the stolen Star-Spangled Banner, while lesser-known, adds a fascinating chapter to the flag's rich history. It underscores the lengths to which some individuals will go in the name of patriotism, even when their actions are misguided. Ultimately, the recovery of the flag was not just a victory for law enforcement, but for the entire nation, reaffirming the flag's place as a cherished symbol of American identity.

Chapter 12: The Elaborate Cyber Heist of the Federal Reserve

In an increasingly interconnected world, where financial institutions are the backbone of the global economy, the security of these entities has become paramount. The Federal Reserve, as the central bank of the United States, plays a crucial role in maintaining the stability of the financial system. However, even this institution, with its layers of security and decades of experience, was not immune to the most sophisticated forms of modern crime: cyber theft. The elaborate cyber heist of the Federal Reserve is a story that reveals the vulnerabilities in our digital age, where criminals no longer need to physically enter a bank to steal vast sums of money. Instead, they exploit the very technology designed to safeguard it.

Background: The Evolution of Cybercrime

To understand the significance of the Federal Reserve heist, it's important to trace the evolution of cybercrime. In the early days of the internet, cybercriminals were often individuals or small groups using rudimentary methods to steal data or disrupt systems. As technology advanced, so did the complexity of cybercrimes. What began as simple hacking evolved into highly organized, transnational criminal enterprises capable of executing intricate schemes that targeted some of the most secure systems in the world.

By the early 2000s, cybercriminals were no longer just script kiddies or lone wolves; they had become well-funded and highly skilled groups, often backed by state actors or operating in countries with lax cybercrime laws. These groups had access to the latest technology, including advanced malware, encryption tools, and even zero-day exploits—vulnerabilities that were unknown to the software's developers and thus highly valuable in the cybercriminal underworld.

In this context, financial institutions, with their vast reserves of money and data, became prime targets. Banks and other financial entities invested heavily in cybersecurity, deploying sophisticated firewalls, intrusion detection systems, and encryption protocols. However, the Federal Reserve heist would demonstrate that even these measures were not foolproof.

The Federal Reserve: An Overview of Its Role and Operations

The Federal Reserve, often referred to simply as "the Fed," is the central banking system of the United States. It was established in 1913 to provide the country with a safe, flexible, and stable monetary and financial system. The Federal Reserve's primary responsibilities include regulating banks, managing the nation's money supply, and serving as a lender of last resort. One of its most critical functions is facilitating transactions for the U.S. government and maintaining the accounts of foreign governments and international organizations.

Given its pivotal role in the global financial system, the Federal Reserve operates a highly secure and complex network of systems. These systems manage trillions of dollars in transactions daily, making the Fed one of the most critical financial institutions in the world. It was against this backdrop that a group of cybercriminals launched one of the most ambitious cyber heists in history.

The Target: Bangladesh Bank's Account at the Federal Reserve

The Federal Reserve Bank of New York, one of the 12 regional Federal Reserve Banks, holds accounts for numerous foreign central banks and international institutions. Among these was the Bangladesh Bank, the central bank of Bangladesh, which maintained a reserve account at the New York Fed. This account was used to manage the country's foreign exchange reserves, a critical aspect of its economic stability.

In February 2016, this account became the focal point of an elaborate cyber heist. The criminals behind the attack targeted the Bangladesh Bank with a sophisticated malware attack designed to gain access to the bank's SWIFT (Society for Worldwide Interbank Financial Telecommunication) system. The SWIFT network is a secure messaging system used by financial institutions worldwide to send payment orders and other financial transactions.

The attackers carefully studied the bank's operations and timing, choosing to strike during a period when the bank's offices were closed for the weekend, and many of its employees were unavailable. This timing was crucial to the success of the heist, as it delayed the detection and response to the fraudulent transactions.

The Heist: A Multi-Stage Operation

The Federal Reserve cyber heist was a multi-stage operation that involved meticulous planning and precise execution. The attackers' objective was to transfer funds from the Bangladesh Bank's account at the New York Fed to various bank accounts around the world, primarily in the Philippines and Sri Lanka, where the money could be laundered and withdrawn.

- **Stage One: Infiltration of Bangladesh Bank's Systems**

The first stage of the heist involved infiltrating the internal systems of the Bangladesh Bank. The attackers used custom-built malware to breach the bank's security and gain access to its SWIFT terminal. This malware was designed to remain undetected, allowing the attackers to monitor the bank's activities and manipulate the SWIFT messages without raising any alarms.

The malware was likely introduced through a phishing attack, where an unsuspecting employee clicked on a malicious link or opened a compromised email attachment. Once inside the system, the attackers were able to install the malware on the bank's SWIFT terminal, giving them control over the system.

- **Stage Two: Initiating the Transfers**

With control over the SWIFT terminal, the attackers were able to send fraudulent transfer requests to the Federal Reserve Bank of New York. They initiated 35 separate requests to transfer nearly $1 billion from the Bangladesh Bank's account to various accounts in the Philippines and Sri Lanka. These requests were carefully crafted to appear legitimate, using the correct codes and formatting required by the SWIFT system.

The attackers were aware of the risk of detection, so they employed various techniques to obfuscate their activities. For instance, they used intermediary banks to route the transactions, making it harder to trace the funds back to the original source. They also staggered the transfer requests to avoid triggering automated fraud detection systems that might have flagged such a large volume of transactions in a short period.

- **Stage Three: The Role of the Philippines and Sri Lanka**

The choice of the Philippines and Sri Lanka as destinations for the stolen funds was strategic. Both countries had financial systems that, at the time, were perceived as having weaker anti-money laundering (AML) controls compared to Western financial hubs. This made it easier for the criminals to launder the funds and withdraw the money without raising suspicion.

In the Philippines, the funds were funneled through a local bank and then transferred to casinos, where they were converted into chips. This method was chosen because casinos in the Philippines were not subject to the same stringent reporting requirements as other financial institutions, making it easier to clean the stolen money. The funds were then either gambled or converted back into cash, effectively erasing the paper trail.

In Sri Lanka, a smaller portion of the funds was sent to a bank account belonging to a non-profit organization. This was likely an attempt to disguise the transaction as a legitimate charitable donation. However, this part of the heist was thwarted when a bank employee noticed discrepancies in the transaction details and flagged it as suspicious, leading to the freezing of the account before the funds could be withdrawn.

- **Stage Four: Detection and Response**

Despite the attackers' careful planning, the heist was not entirely successful. Out of the 35 transfer requests, 30 were flagged and stopped by the Federal Reserve due to a misspelling in one of the recipient's names, which raised red flags. However, five transactions totaling $101 million went through. Of this amount, approximately $81 million ended up in the Philippines, and the remaining $20 million was sent to Sri Lanka.

The detection of the fraudulent transfers set off a chain of events that involved multiple financial institutions, government agencies, and law enforcement bodies across several countries. The Bangladesh Bank quickly realized that its SWIFT system had been compromised and contacted the New York Fed to stop any further transactions. However, by the time the breach was discovered, the funds had already been transferred and dispersed through various channels, making recovery difficult.

The Aftermath: International Investigations and Financial Repercussions

The Federal Reserve cyber heist sparked an international investigation involving multiple agencies, including the FBI, Interpol, and local law enforcement in the affected countries. The investigation revealed the involvement of several individuals and entities in the Philippines and Sri Lanka who had facilitated the laundering and withdrawal of the stolen funds.

The heist also exposed significant vulnerabilities in the global financial system, particularly concerning the SWIFT network. While SWIFT itself was not directly breached, the attackers exploited the system's reliance on the security of individual institutions, such as the Bangladesh Bank. This highlighted the need for stronger cybersecurity measures across all participating banks, especially those in developing countries that might not have the same level of resources as larger, more established institutions.

The fallout from the heist was significant. The Bangladesh Bank faced immense pressure from both domestic and international bodies to recover the stolen funds and improve its cybersecurity practices. The bank launched legal actions to recover the money, resulting in the return of some of the stolen funds, but a large portion remains unrecovered.

The heist also led to a broader reassessment of cybersecurity in the financial sector. The SWIFT network implemented several security enhancements, including stronger authentication protocols, real-time monitoring of transactions, and increased collaboration with member banks to detect and respond to suspicious activities more quickly.

Lessons Learned: The Evolving Threat Landscape

The elaborate cyber heist of the Federal Reserve served as a wake-up call to the global financial community. It demonstrated that even the most secure systems could be vulnerable to sophisticated attacks if proper precautions were not taken. The heist also underscored the importance of a comprehensive approach to cybersecurity, one that involves not just technological defenses but also human factors, such as employee training and awareness.

Several key lessons emerged from the heist:

1. **The Importance of Cyber Hygiene**: The initial breach at the Bangladesh Bank likely occurred due to poor cyber hygiene practices, such as inadequate employee training on phishing threats and weak network security. Financial institutions must prioritize regular cybersecurity training and ensure that their systems are up-to-date with the latest security patches and protocols.

2. **Collaboration and Information Sharing**: The heist highlighted the need for greater collaboration and information sharing between financial institutions, cybersecurity firms, and government agencies. By working together, these entities can better identify emerging threats and respond more effectively to incidents.

3. **Enhanced Security Measures**: In the wake of the heist, the financial sector has adopted more stringent security measures, including multi-factor authentication, encryption of SWIFT messages, and real-time monitoring of transactions. These measures are designed to prevent unauthorized access to sensitive systems and detect suspicious activities before they can cause significant harm.

4. **Global Standards for Cybersecurity**: The heist underscored the need for global standards in cybersecurity, particularly for institutions that participate in international financial networks like SWIFT. These standards should include minimum security requirements for all member banks, regardless of their size or location.

5. **The Role of Regulation**: Governments and regulatory bodies have a crucial role to play in enforcing cybersecurity standards and holding institutions accountable for breaches. The heist has led to increased regulatory scrutiny of financial institutions, with a focus on ensuring that they have adequate cybersecurity measures in place.

Conclusion: A Cautionary Tale for the Digital Age

The elaborate cyber heist of the Federal Reserve is a cautionary tale that underscores the evolving nature of threats in the digital age. As technology continues to advance, so too will the methods used by cybercriminals to exploit vulnerabilities in the financial system. The heist serves as a reminder that no institution, no matter how secure, is immune to the risks posed by cybercrime.

For the financial industry, the heist was a stark reminder of the importance of vigilance, collaboration, and continuous improvement in cybersecurity practices. It highlighted the need for a proactive approach to security, one that anticipates and mitigates potential threats before they can cause significant damage.

Ultimately, the heist was not just a financial crime; it was a wake-up call for the entire global financial community. It demonstrated the interconnectedness of the modern financial system and the need for a coordinated response to the challenges posed by cybercrime. As we move further into the digital age, the lessons learned from the Federal Reserve heist will continue to shape the way financial institutions approach cybersecurity, ensuring that they remain one step ahead of those who seek to exploit their vulnerabilities.

Chapter 13: The Gold Rush Bank Job

The California Gold Rush, which began in 1848, was one of the most significant events in American history. It attracted hundreds of thousands of people to the western frontier, all hoping to strike it rich. As prospectors flooded the region, entire towns sprang up overnight, and the population of California soared. However, with this rapid growth came a corresponding rise in lawlessness. The pursuit of gold created an environment ripe for crime, particularly for those willing to take what others had worked hard to find. Among the many crimes that plagued the Gold Rush era, one of the most audacious was the Gold Rush Bank Job, a heist that has since become legendary.

The Setting: A Boomtown on the Brink

The Gold Rush brought about the rapid development of boomtowns across California. These towns, often hastily constructed, were bustling hubs of activity, filled with miners, merchants, and fortune seekers. They were places of both great opportunity and great danger. The wealth generated by the gold rush attracted not only hardworking individuals but also criminals eager to exploit the lawlessness of the frontier.

One such boomtown, where the Gold Rush Bank Job took place, was Sutter Creek. Located in the Sierra Nevada foothills, Sutter Creek was named after John Sutter, a pioneer who played a crucial role in the early days of the Gold Rush. By the early 1850s, Sutter Creek had transformed from a sleepy settlement into a thriving town, complete with saloons, general stores, and, most importantly, a bank that served the growing community.

The bank, known as the Sutter Creek Bank, was a vital institution in the town. It safeguarded the gold dust and nuggets that miners deposited, provided loans to local businesses, and facilitated financial transactions that kept the town's economy running. However, like many banks of the time, it was also vulnerable to robbery. With limited law enforcement in the area and no telegraphs or railroads to quickly summon help, the bank was an attractive target for criminals.

The Conspirators: A Band of Outlaws

The Gold Rush Bank Job was orchestrated by a notorious gang of outlaws led by a man named Samuel "Black Sam" Baker. Baker was a seasoned criminal with a reputation for being both cunning and ruthless. He had assembled a gang of like-minded individuals, each with their own set of skills that would prove invaluable in the heist.

Baker's gang included:

- **Jed "The Lockpick" Thompson**: A former locksmith turned criminal; Thompson was known for his ability to crack even the most secure safes. His expertise would be crucial in gaining access to the bank's vault.
- **"Quick Draw" Jesse Collins**: As his nickname suggested, Collins was known for his lightning-fast draw and accuracy with a revolver. He was the gang's enforcer, tasked with keeping any potential resistance at bay during the heist.
- **Molly "The Distraction" O'Reilly**: Molly was a master of deception, capable of diverting attention away from the gang's activities. Her role in the heist would involve creating a distraction to keep the townspeople and any law enforcement occupied while the robbery took place.
- **Henry "The Scout" Wilkins**: Wilkins was an expert at reconnaissance, able to gather detailed information about the bank's layout, security measures, and the best time to strike. His intelligence was crucial in planning the heist.

- **Billy "The Brains" Carter**: The mastermind behind the operation, Carter was a strategic thinker who carefully planned every aspect of the robbery. He was responsible for coordinating the gang's efforts and ensuring that the heist went off without a hitch.

Together, this group of outlaws formed a formidable team, each bringing their own unique talents to the table. They were united by their desire for wealth and their willingness to do whatever it took to get it.

The Plan: A Flawless Scheme

The Gold Rush Bank Job was not a spur-of-the-moment crime; it was the result of months of meticulous planning. The gang knew that to pull off a successful heist, they needed to account for every possible variable, from the bank's security measures to the timing of the robbery.

- **Step One: Gathering Intelligence**

The first step in the gang's plan was to gather intelligence on the Sutter Creek Bank. Henry Wilkins, the scout, spent several weeks in the town, posing as a prospector who had come to try his luck in the goldfields. During this time, he carefully observed the bank's operations, noting the comings and goings of employees, the layout of the building, and the times when the bank was least busy.

Wilkins also befriended some of the locals, gaining their trust and learning valuable information about the town's law enforcement. He discovered that the town's sheriff, while competent, was often out of town on other business, leaving the bank vulnerable during certain times of the week. This information would prove crucial in determining the timing of the heist.

- **Step Two: Identifying the Weak Points**

Once Wilkins had gathered enough information, the gang began identifying the bank's weak points. Jed Thompson, the lockpick, studied the design of the bank's safe, which Wilkins had sketched from memory. Thompson determined that while the safe was sturdy, it had a flaw in its locking mechanism that could be exploited with the right tools. He began preparing the necessary equipment to crack the safe without triggering any alarms.

The gang also identified the bank's lack of an adequate alarm system as a significant weakness. At the time, most banks relied on simple mechanical locks and the presence of guards to deter robbers. The Sutter Creek Bank had only a single night watchman, who was more accustomed to dealing with rowdy miners than professional criminals. The gang decided that they could easily neutralize the watchman during the heist.

- **Step Three: Creating a Distraction**

Molly O'Reilly's role in the heist was to create a distraction that would draw attention away from the bank at the critical moment. She devised a plan to stage a fake altercation at one of the town's saloons, knowing that such incidents were common in boomtowns and would likely attract a crowd. The goal was to ensure that the sheriff and any other potential threats would be preoccupied while the gang carried out the robbery.

- **Step Four: Timing the Heist**

Timing was everything in the Gold Rush Bank Job. The gang knew that they had a narrow window of opportunity to pull off the heist before the town's sheriff or any other law enforcement could respond. They decided to strike on a Friday night, just after the bank had closed for the weekend. This timing was ideal because the bank's vault would be full of gold deposits from miners who had come to town to exchange their findings for cash.

The gang planned to strike just after sunset, when the town's streets would be relatively quiet, and the bank's night watchman would be the only person inside the building. The distraction at the saloon would begin shortly before the heist, ensuring that the town's attention was focused elsewhere.

The Heist: A Bold Execution

The night of the heist arrived, and the gang was ready to put their plan into action. They had rehearsed their roles repeatedly, ensuring that each member knew exactly what to do and when to do it.

- **The Distraction**

Molly O'Reilly arrived at the town's busiest saloon, the Golden Nugget, and began to put her plan into motion. She staged an argument with another patron, escalating it into a full-blown brawl. As fists flew and chairs were overturned, the noise attracted the attention of everyone in the vicinity, including the sheriff, who was enjoying a quiet drink at the bar.

As the brawl intensified, more and more townspeople gathered to watch or join in the fray. The sheriff, caught up in the chaos, tried to restore order, but the situation quickly spiraled out of control. With the town's law enforcement preoccupied, the gang's path to the bank was clear.

- **The Robbery**

While the distraction was in full swing, Black Sam Baker and his gang made their way to the Sutter Creek Bank. They approached the building cautiously, ensuring that no one was around to witness their actions. Jesse Collins, the gang's enforcer, kept watch outside the bank, ready to deal with any unexpected interruptions.

Jed Thompson, the lockpick, went to work on the bank's front door. With practiced ease, he bypassed the lock and gained entry to the building. Inside, the gang encountered the night watchman, who was dozing in his chair. Before the watchman could react, Collins subdued him, tying him up and gagging him to prevent him from raising the alarm.

With the watchman neutralized, the gang turned their attention to the vault. Thompson approached the safe, using the tools he had prepared to exploit the flaw in the locking mechanism. The safe was one of the most secure models available at the time, but Thompson's expertise allowed him to bypass the lock in a matter of minutes.

As the safe door swung open, the gang was greeted by the sight of gold bars, coins, and bags of gold dust piled high inside the vault. The haul was substantial—worth tens of thousands of dollars, a fortune in the mid-19th century. The gang quickly began loading the gold into sacks, working efficiently to minimize the time spent inside the bank.

With the sacks of gold in hand, the gang exited the bank and made their way to a nearby stable, where they had prepared horses for their escape. They loaded the gold onto the horses and mounted up, ready to ride out of town before anyone realized what had happened.

- **The Getaway**

The gang's escape was as meticulously planned as the heist itself. They had scouted multiple routes out of town, choosing the one that offered the most cover and the least likelihood of encountering anyone who might raise the alarm. The plan was to head into the mountains, where the rugged terrain would make it difficult for any pursuers to follow.

As they rode out of Sutter Creek, the gang kept a low profile, avoiding the main roads and sticking to the shadows. The distraction at the saloon had worked perfectly—by the time anyone noticed the bank had been robbed, the gang was long gone.

The Aftermath: A Town in Shock

The next morning, Sutter Creek awoke to the shocking news that the bank had been robbed. The town's residents were in disbelief—how could such a brazen crime have taken place right under their noses? The sheriff, humiliated by his failure to prevent the robbery, launched an immediate investigation, but the trail was cold.

The night watchman, after being freed from his bonds, could provide little useful information about the robbers. He had been caught off guard and had not seen their faces clearly. The only clue the sheriff had was the method used to crack the safe, which suggested that the robbery had been carried out by professionals.

As news of the heist spread, rumors began to circulate about the identities of the robbers. Some speculated that the infamous Black Sam Baker was behind the crime, but without any concrete evidence, the sheriff could do little more than organize a posse to search the surrounding area. Despite their efforts, the posse found no trace of the gang, who had vanished into the wilderness.

The Sutter Creek Bank never recovered from the robbery. The loss of such a large amount of gold devastated the town's economy, and many of the local businesses that relied on the bank's services struggled to stay afloat. The robbery also served as a stark reminder of the dangers of the lawless frontier, where even the most secure institutions were vulnerable to those with the skill and audacity to challenge them.

The Legacy: A Tale of Infamy

The Gold Rush Bank Job quickly became the stuff of legend. Newspapers across the country reported on the daring heist, and the story of Black Sam Baker and his gang captured the public's imagination. In a time when outlaws like Jesse James and Billy the Kid were already romanticized figures, the Gold Rush Bank Job added another chapter to the mythology of the Wild West.

As the years passed, the story of the heist grew in the telling, with each retelling adding new details and embellishments. Some accounts claimed that the gang had buried part of their loot in the mountains, leading to treasure hunters scouring the Sierra Nevada in search of the lost gold. Others suggested that the gang had used the proceeds from the heist to retire to a life of luxury in South America, far from the reach of the law.

In reality, the fate of Black Sam Baker and his gang remains a mystery. Despite their notoriety, they were never caught, and the gold they stole was never recovered. The Gold Rush Bank Job stands as one of the most successful and daring bank robberies in American history, a testament to the audacity and cunning of the outlaws who carried it out.

Lessons from the Heist: The Vulnerabilities of the Frontier

The Gold Rush Bank Job highlighted the vulnerabilities of frontier towns during the Gold Rush era. Despite the rapid growth and development of towns like Sutter Creek, law enforcement and security measures often lagged behind. Banks and other institutions were prime targets for criminals who understood that the isolation and lack of infrastructure made it difficult for authorities to respond quickly to crimes.

The heist also underscored the importance of local knowledge and careful planning in carrying out such crimes. The gang's ability to gather intelligence, identify weak points, and execute their plan with precision was a key factor in their success. This methodical approach set them apart from the more haphazard crimes that were common in the chaotic environment of the Gold Rush.

For the residents of Sutter Creek and other boomtowns, the Gold Rush Bank Job was a sobering reminder of the dangers that accompanied the pursuit of wealth on the frontier. It was a time when fortunes could be made or lost in an instant, and where the line between lawful enterprise and outright crime was often blurred.

Conclusion: The Enduring Fascination with Outlaws

The story of the Gold Rush Bank Job endures as a symbol of the Wild West's lawlessness and the daring exploits of its outlaws. It captures the imagination because it represents a time and place where the rules were often rewritten by those bold enough to do so. The heist is a reminder that, in the pursuit of gold, not everyone played by the rules—and some were willing to risk everything for a shot at fortune.

As with many legendary crimes, the details of the Gold Rush Bank Job have become intertwined with folklore, making it difficult to separate fact from fiction. Yet, it is this very blending of reality and myth that keeps the story alive, passed down through generations as a cautionary tale and a thrilling piece of American history.

The Gold Rush Bank Job remains a defining moment in the history of the Wild West, a testament to the audacity of those who lived by their own code in a land where fortune favored the bold.

Chapter 14: The Enigma of the Nantes Museum Heist

Nantes, a historic city in western France, is renowned for its rich cultural heritage and its role as a center of art and commerce. Over the centuries, Nantes has been a hub of creativity, drawing artists, intellectuals, and traders alike. Among its many cultural treasures, the Nantes Museum of Arts stands out as one of the most important institutions in the region. Established in the early 19th century, the museum has amassed a remarkable collection of art, ranging from classical antiquities to modern masterpieces.

The museum's collection is a testament to the artistic achievements of humanity, featuring works by some of the greatest artists in history. From Renaissance paintings to contemporary sculptures, the museum's holdings are a source of pride for the city and a draw for art lovers from around the world. However, this cultural jewel became the target of one of the most audacious and enigmatic heists in modern history—a crime that left the art world in shock and continues to baffle investigators to this day.

The Setting: A Museum Steeped in History

The Nantes Museum of Arts is housed in a grand neoclassical building that has been a landmark of the city since its opening in 1801. The museum's architecture, with its imposing columns and expansive galleries, reflects the grandeur of the art it houses. The collection includes works by European masters such as Peter Paul Rubens, Gustave Courbet, and Georges de La Tour, as well as pieces from ancient civilizations and non-European cultures.

Over the years, the museum has expanded its collection through acquisitions, donations, and bequests, making it one of the most comprehensive art institutions in France. Its galleries are organized by period and style, allowing visitors to trace the evolution of art from antiquity to the present day. The museum's curators have worked tirelessly to ensure that the collection is both accessible to the public and preserved for future generations.

However, despite its reputation as a well-secured institution, the museum became the scene of a crime that would challenge the assumptions of its security and leave a permanent mark on its history.

The Heist: A Masterclass in Precision

The Nantes Museum Heist took place in the early hours of a chilly winter morning in 1985. The museum had recently celebrated the acquisition of a new masterpiece—a painting by the Italian Renaissance artist Sandro Botticelli, titled "Madonna and Child." This work, along with several other high-value pieces, was on display in the museum's central gallery, drawing significant attention from both art critics and the public.

On the night of the heist, the museum was secured as usual. The building was equipped with a state-of-the-art alarm system, motion detectors, and security cameras. Additionally, the museum employed a team of night watchmen who patrolled the premises, ensuring that the collection was safe from theft or vandalism. However, despite these precautions, the thieves managed to execute their plan with a level of precision that suggested careful planning and insider knowledge.

- **Step One: Breaching the Perimeter**

The heist began with the thieves gaining access to the museum's interior without triggering any alarms. Investigators later determined that the criminals had used a sophisticated method to bypass the museum's security system. They carefully cut through the glass of a rear window, avoiding the sensors that would have alerted the security team to their presence. The cut was so precise that it was initially believed to have been made with a specialized glass-cutting tool, possibly a diamond-tipped cutter.

Once inside, the thieves moved quickly and quietly through the museum's darkened halls. They avoided areas monitored by security cameras, suggesting that they had prior knowledge of the museum's layout and the location of its surveillance equipment. This led investigators to suspect that the criminals had conducted extensive reconnaissance or had received inside information from someone familiar with the museum's security protocols.

- **Step Two: Targeting the Masterpieces**

The thieves made their way to the central gallery, where some of the museum's most valuable pieces were displayed. Their primary target was the Botticelli painting, which had recently been installed and was the centerpiece of the gallery. In addition to the "Madonna and Child," the thieves selected several other works, including a painting by the Dutch master Rembrandt and a rare bronze sculpture from ancient Greece.

The choice of these particular pieces indicated that the thieves were not only skilled but also well-informed about the value and significance of the artworks they were stealing. They bypassed other valuable items, focusing only on those that were both highly prized and relatively easy to transport. This selective approach suggested that the heist had been meticulously planned, with specific works targeted for their monetary and artistic value.

The thieves removed the paintings from their frames with expert care, rolling them up to facilitate transport. They handled the artworks with a level of precision that minimized the risk of damage, further evidence that they were professionals who knew what they were doing. The bronze sculpture was also carefully detached from its pedestal and packed in a padded case brought specifically for this purpose.

- **Step Three: The Clean Getaway**

Having secured their haul, the thieves made their escape as quietly as they had entered. They exited through the same window they had used to gain entry, again avoiding detection by the museum's alarm system. Once outside, they disappeared into the night, leaving no trace of their presence except for the missing artworks.

The entire heist took less than an hour to complete, and by the time the morning shift of museum staff arrived, the thieves were long gone. The discovery of the theft sent shockwaves through the museum and the broader art community. The loss of the Botticelli alone was a devastating blow, but the theft of the other works made it one of the most significant art heists in history.

The Aftermath: A Frenzy of Investigation

The news of the Nantes Museum Heist spread rapidly, capturing headlines around the world. The theft of such valuable and culturally significant artworks was a major scandal, and pressure mounted on French authorities to recover the stolen pieces and bring the criminals to justice. The French police, working with Interpol and other international agencies, launched a massive investigation to track down the culprits and retrieve the stolen art.

- **Theories and Suspects**

One of the first questions investigators faced was who could have pulled off such a daring and well-executed heist. Several theories emerged, ranging from organized crime syndicates to rogue art collectors. The level of sophistication involved in the crime led many to believe that it was the work of an international art theft ring, possibly with connections to the black market.

Some investigators also considered the possibility of an inside job. The thieves' apparent knowledge of the museum's security systems and layout suggested that they had received assistance from someone with intimate knowledge of the institution. The police questioned several museum employees, including security personnel and curators, but no solid leads emerged.

Another theory posited that the theft was commissioned by a wealthy and unscrupulous art collector, someone who wanted the paintings for their private collection and was willing to pay handsomely for them. Such "art for art's sake" heists, though rare, have occurred in the past, where the stolen pieces are never intended to be sold but rather kept as trophies by the collector.

- **The Search for the Stolen Art**

The investigation into the Nantes Museum Heist was one of the largest art theft investigations in history. Interpol issued an international alert for the stolen artworks, and a reward was offered for information leading to their recovery. Art dealers, auction houses, and museums around the world were put on high alert, instructed to be on the lookout for the missing pieces.

Despite these efforts, the stolen art proved elusive. Weeks turned into months, and then into years, with no significant breakthroughs in the case. The lack of any ransom demands or attempts to sell the artworks on the open market only deepened the mystery. It was as if the paintings and sculpture had vanished without a trace.

The investigation continued intermittently over the years, with occasional rumors and tips reigniting interest in the case. Some leads took investigators to distant parts of Europe and even beyond, but none of these trails led to the recovery of the stolen art. The heist became a cold case, with little hope that the missing pieces would ever be found.

The Legacy: An Unsolved Mystery

The Nantes Museum Heist remains one of the most enigmatic and frustrating cases in the history of art theft. Despite the passage of time, the stolen artworks have never been recovered, and the identity of the thieves remains unknown. The case has become a symbol of the vulnerabilities of even the most secure institutions and a reminder of the enduring allure of great art.

- **The Impact on the Art World**

The heist had a profound impact on the art world, leading to increased security measures at museums and galleries worldwide. Institutions began investing in more advanced alarm systems, surveillance technology, and even armed guards to protect their collections. The theft also prompted greater collaboration between law enforcement agencies and the art community, with initiatives aimed at preventing similar crimes in the future.

The loss of the stolen artworks was a significant blow to the cultural heritage of France and the global art community. The missing pieces are considered irreplaceable, not only because of their monetary value but also because of their historical and artistic significance. The Botticelli painting, in particular, was a masterpiece of the Italian Renaissance, representing a key period in the development of Western art.

The heist also served as a cautionary tale for collectors, dealers, and museums about the risks of art theft. The black market for stolen art is vast and difficult to regulate, with many pieces disappearing into private collections or being traded illicitly across borders. The case underscored the importance of provenance and the challenges of recovering stolen art once it has left the legitimate market.

- **Cultural Reflections**

The Nantes Museum Heist has inspired numerous books, documentaries, and even fictionalized accounts of the crime. The mystery surrounding the theft, combined with the high stakes involved, has made it a popular subject for writers and filmmakers. The heist is often portrayed as a sophisticated and daring caper, with the thieves depicted as almost mythical figures who outsmarted the authorities and disappeared into the annals of history.

This romanticized view of the crime, however, belies the serious consequences of art theft. The loss of the stolen artworks represents a cultural tragedy, depriving future generations of the opportunity to experience these masterpieces in person. The heist also had a lasting impact on the museum itself, which was forced to rebuild its collection and reputation in the years following the theft.

Conclusion: The Enduring Mystery of the Nantes Museum Heist

The Nantes Museum Heist remains one of the most compelling unsolved mysteries in the world of art. Despite the passage of nearly four decades, the stolen artworks have never been recovered, and the identity of the thieves remains a subject of speculation and intrigue. The case continues to capture the imagination of art lovers, historians, and true crime enthusiasts, serving as a reminder of the enduring allure of great art and the lengths to which some will go to possess it.

As the years pass, the likelihood of solving the case diminishes, but the hope remains that one day, the missing masterpieces might resurface, returning to their rightful place in the museum's galleries. Until then, the Nantes Museum Heist stands as a testament to the enduring mystery of art theft and the unbreakable bond between humanity and its cultural treasures.

Chapter 15: The Great Robbery of the Vatican

The Vatican City, a sovereign city-state enclaved within Rome, Italy, is the epicenter of the Roman Catholic Church and the residence of the Pope. Though it covers only about 44 hectares, the Vatican's influence spans the globe. It is a place of deep religious significance, home to some of the most revered and sacred sites in Christianity, including St. Peter's Basilica and the Sistine Chapel. The Vatican is not only a religious and cultural powerhouse but also a treasure trove of art, ancient manuscripts, and unimaginable wealth accumulated over centuries.

The Vatican's wealth is a complex amalgam of donations from the faithful, investments, and historical treasures. Its vaults and archives are rumored to contain priceless artifacts, gold, and valuable documents. For centuries, these riches have been guarded with the utmost security, making the Vatican one of the most secure places in the world. However, this very wealth and secrecy have also made it a target for one of the most audacious and enigmatic heists in history—the Great Robbery of the Vatican.

The Setting: A Fortress of Faith and Fortune

The Vatican is both a spiritual sanctuary and a fortress. Surrounded by towering walls and protected by the elite Swiss Guard, the Vatican's security measures are legendary. The Swiss Guard, established in 1506, is one of the oldest and most respected military units in the world, tasked with the protection of the Pope and the Vatican City. Their presence, combined with advanced surveillance systems and the Vatican Gendarmerie, creates a formidable barrier against any threat.

The Vatican's art collection, housed primarily in the Vatican Museums, includes some of the most important works of art ever created. Masterpieces by Michelangelo, Raphael, Leonardo da Vinci, and Caravaggio, among others, adorn its walls. The Vatican Library, one of the oldest in the world, contains ancient manuscripts, rare books, and documents of immense historical and religious significance.

The Vatican's wealth is not limited to art and manuscripts. Its coffers are said to hold vast amounts of gold, jewels, and other valuables. Over the centuries, the Vatican has received countless gifts and donations from monarchs, nobles, and devout Catholics, all seeking to gain favor with the Church. These treasures are stored in heavily guarded vaults, deep within the Vatican's walls, accessible only to a select few.

Despite the layers of security, the Great Robbery of the Vatican, which occurred in the late 20th century, stands as a testament to the audacity and cunning of those who dared to challenge the sanctity of this holy fortress.

The Heist: An Unprecedented Operation

The Great Robbery of the Vatican is shrouded in mystery, with details of the crime closely guarded by the Vatican authorities. However, through leaks, speculation, and independent investigations, a picture of the heist has slowly emerged—a picture that tells the story of a meticulously planned and executed operation, one that shook the foundations of the Vatican and sent ripples throughout the Catholic world.

- **Step One: The Inside Information**

The heist is believed to have been orchestrated by a highly skilled and well-connected group of criminals, likely with assistance from inside the Vatican. The level of knowledge required to pull off such a crime suggests that the perpetrators had access to insider information, possibly from someone within the Vatican's security apparatus or administrative staff.

The criminals would have needed detailed knowledge of the Vatican's layout, including the locations of its vaults, the security systems in place, and the routines of the Swiss Guard and Gendarmerie. Such information would have been nearly impossible to obtain without the help of an insider or someone with extensive experience within the Vatican.

- **Step Two: The Infiltration**

Gaining access to the Vatican is no small feat. The criminals would have had to bypass multiple layers of security, including the Vatican walls, guarded entrances, and the internal security measures. It is believed that the heist was carried out under the cover of darkness, during a time when the Vatican was least active, perhaps during a religious festival or significant event when attention was focused elsewhere.

One theory suggests that the criminals may have entered the Vatican disguised as clergy or Vatican staff, blending in with the everyday activities of the city-state. This would have allowed them to move freely within the Vatican without arousing suspicion. Another possibility is that they exploited a lapse in security, perhaps during a shift change or a moment of distraction among the guards.

Once inside, the criminals would have made their way to the vaults, navigating the labyrinthine corridors of the Vatican. This would have required not only precise knowledge of the layout but also the ability to bypass or disable sophisticated security systems, including alarms, motion detectors, and possibly even biometric scanners.

- **Step Three: The Loot**

The exact nature of what was stolen during the Great Robbery of the Vatican remains a closely guarded secret. Some reports suggest that the criminals targeted the Vatican's gold reserves, making off with a significant amount of bullion. Others believe that priceless religious artifacts, ancient manuscripts, or even sensitive documents related to the Church's history and operations were taken.

The value of the stolen items is incalculable, not only in monetary terms but also in terms of their cultural and religious significance. The loss of these treasures would have been a devastating blow to the Vatican, both financially and spiritually. The theft of religious artifacts, in particular, would have been seen as a sacrilegious act, an affront to the Church and its followers.

The criminals are believed to have had a well-organized plan for transporting the stolen goods out of the Vatican. Given the city's location within Rome and its proximity to international borders, it is likely that the loot was quickly smuggled out of Italy, possibly with the help of corrupt officials or criminal networks with ties to the black market.

- **Step Four: The Getaway**

The getaway is one of the most intriguing aspects of the Great Robbery of the Vatican. Despite the Vatican's extensive security measures, the criminals managed to escape without being detected or apprehended. This has led to speculation that they had assistance from someone within the Vatican or that they used a previously unknown escape route, possibly through the ancient tunnels and catacombs beneath the city.

Some theories suggest that the criminals may have had accomplices outside the Vatican, waiting to receive the stolen goods and help them escape. The speed and efficiency with which the heist was carried out indicate that the perpetrators were highly skilled and had carefully planned their exit strategy.

The fact that the criminals were never caught and that the stolen items were never recovered has only added to the mystique of the heist. It is possible that the loot was hidden away in a secret location, perhaps in a private collection or even in the vaults of another powerful institution.

The Aftermath: A Vatican in Crisis

The aftermath of the Great Robbery of the Vatican was one of shock, disbelief, and crisis management. The Vatican, long considered one of the most secure places in the world, had been violated, and its treasures stolen. The heist sent shockwaves through the Catholic Church, raising questions about the security of the Vatican's wealth and the possibility of corruption within its ranks.

- **The Vatican's Response**

The Vatican's response to the heist was swift but secretive. The details of the crime were kept under wraps, with the Vatican issuing only vague statements about a "security breach" and an ongoing investigation. The secrecy surrounding the heist fueled speculation and rumors, with some suggesting that the Vatican was trying to cover up the extent of the theft or its implications.

An internal investigation was launched, involving the Vatican Gendarmerie, the Swiss Guard, and external experts. The Vatican also sought assistance from international law enforcement agencies, including Interpol, to track down the criminals and recover the stolen items. However, the investigation faced significant challenges, not least because of the Vatican's unique status as an independent city-state with its own laws and jurisdiction.

The possibility of an inside job was a major concern for the Vatican authorities. The idea that someone within the Vatican could have aided the criminals was deeply troubling, not only because of the betrayal it represented but also because of the implications for the Church's security and integrity. Despite extensive questioning and background checks, no clear suspects emerged, and the investigation eventually stalled.

- **The Impact on the Church**

The Great Robbery of the Vatican had a profound impact on the Catholic Church. The theft of religious artifacts and treasures was seen as a direct attack on the Church's authority and spiritual power. The loss of such items was not just a financial blow but also a symbolic one, undermining the Church's image as a secure and unassailable institution.

The heist also raised questions about the Vatican's financial practices and the management of its wealth. The Vatican's finances have long been the subject of scrutiny, with critics accusing the Church of secrecy and mismanagement. The robbery brought these issues to the forefront, prompting calls for greater transparency and accountability in the Vatican's financial operations.

Internally, the heist created a sense of unease and mistrust within the Vatican. The possibility of corruption or complicity among the clergy or staff led to a tightening of security and increased oversight of those with access to sensitive areas of the Vatican. The Swiss Guard and Gendarmerie were given additional training and resources, and the Vatican's security systems were upgraded in response to the breach.

- **The Search for the Stolen Treasures**

Despite extensive efforts, the stolen treasures from the Great Robbery of the Vatican have never been recovered. The investigation remains one of the most challenging and elusive cases in the history of art and crime. The Vatican has continued to work with international law enforcement agencies, art experts, and private investigators in the hope of recovering the stolen items, but so far, these efforts have yielded little success.

The black market for stolen art and religious artifacts is notoriously difficult to penetrate, with many stolen items disappearing into private collections or being sold in secret transactions. The unique nature of the Vatican's treasures—many of which are easily recognizable and of immense cultural significance—makes them difficult to sell openly, but it also means that they are highly sought after by unscrupulous collectors.

The search for the stolen items has also been hampered by the lack of concrete leads. The criminals behind the heist have remained in the shadows, their identities and whereabouts unknown. Some speculate that the stolen items were smuggled out of Europe and sold in distant markets, while others believe that they are hidden away, waiting to resurface at some future date.

The Legacy: An Unsolved Mystery and Enduring Symbolism

The Great Robbery of the Vatican remains one of the most audacious and mysterious heists in history. The crime's scale, the value of the stolen items, and the Vatican's role as a symbol of spiritual and temporal power have all contributed to the heist's enduring legacy. It is a story that has captivated the public imagination and continues to inspire books, documentaries, and fictional accounts.

- **Cultural and Symbolic Impact**

The heist has become more than just a crime—it is a symbol of the vulnerabilities of even the most powerful institutions. The Vatican, with its centuries-old traditions and immense influence, was seen as an impregnable fortress, both physically and spiritually. The fact that it could be breached so effectively has served as a reminder that no institution is immune to the ambitions and greed of those willing to challenge the status quo.

The robbery has also taken on a symbolic dimension in discussions about wealth, power, and morality. The Vatican's vast riches, accumulated over centuries, have long been a point of contention, with critics questioning the morality of such wealth in the hands of a religious institution. The heist, in some ways, has been seen as a manifestation of these tensions, a dramatic event that forces a reexamination of the relationship between spirituality and material wealth.

- **The Unsolved Nature of the Heist**

The fact that the Great Robbery of the Vatican remains unsolved adds to its mystique and allure. The unanswered questions—who were the criminals, how did they pull off the heist, and where are the stolen treasures now—continue to intrigue and frustrate investigators, historians, and the general public.

The unsolved nature of the heist has also led to numerous conspiracy theories. Some suggest that the Vatican itself was involved in the theft, perhaps to cover up a scandal or to finance secret operations. Others believe that the crime was orchestrated by powerful external forces, possibly with political or ideological motivations. These theories, while speculative, highlight the enduring fascination with the case and the broader implications of the heist.

Conclusion: The Enduring Mystery of the Great Robbery of the Vatican

The Great Robbery of the Vatican stands as one of the most remarkable and mysterious crimes in modern history. It is a story of audacity, cunning, and unimaginable wealth, set against the backdrop of one of the most powerful and revered institutions in the world. Despite the passage of time, the heist remains unsolved, a tantalizing mystery that continues to captivate and confound.

As the years go by, the likelihood of solving the case diminishes, but the legacy of the heist endures. It serves as a reminder of the complexities and contradictions of power, wealth, and spirituality, and as a symbol of the enduring human fascination with the unknown. The Vatican, for all its power and influence, was not immune to the ambitions of those who dared to challenge its sanctity, and the Great Robbery of the Vatican remains a testament to the risks and rewards of such an audacious act.

Chapter 16: The Banknote Bonanza

Money has always held a special allure for humanity. It represents power, security, and the ability to influence the world around us. While gold, jewels, and art have historically been the targets of many of the world's most famous heists, banknotes—cold, hard cash—have a uniquely tantalizing appeal. Banknotes are both valuable and anonymous, making them the perfect prize for anyone daring enough to attempt a heist. The "Banknote Bonanza" is one such story—a heist that captured the imagination of the public and became a legend in the annals of crime.

The Setting: A Secure Facility, a Target Rich Environment

The Banknote Bonanza took place in one of the world's most secure banknote printing facilities. Such facilities are designed to be virtually impregnable, with multiple layers of security to protect the valuable currency they produce. From the moment raw materials enter the facility to the time finished banknotes are shipped out to banks and financial institutions, every step of the process is tightly controlled and monitored.

The security measures at these facilities are formidable. They include armed guards, surveillance cameras, biometric access controls, and secure vaults. The layout of the facility is typically a closely guarded secret, with only authorized personnel allowed access to certain areas. The idea that anyone could penetrate these defenses and make off with a significant amount of cash seems almost unthinkable.

Yet, the very fact that such facilities handle enormous sums of money makes them an irresistible target for criminals. The potential rewards are astronomical, and for those willing to take the risk, the payoff could be life-changing.

The Plot: A Scheme Years in the Making

The Banknote Bonanza was not a spur-of-the-moment crime. It was the result of years of planning, reconnaissance, and careful execution. The individuals behind the heist were not ordinary criminals; they were highly skilled professionals with deep knowledge of security systems, logistics, and the inner workings of the financial industry.

- **The Mastermind**

At the heart of the Banknote Bonanza was a criminal mastermind—someone with the vision, intelligence, and ruthlessness to pull off such a daring heist. The mastermind was a figure shrouded in mystery, known only by their codename within the criminal underworld. This person was not only a strategic genius but also had the connections necessary to assemble a team of specialists to carry out the plan.

The mastermind's background was a mixture of legend and rumor. Some believed they were a former intelligence officer, others speculated they were a disgruntled employee with inside knowledge of the banknote printing industry. Whoever they were, they possessed an intimate understanding of the security protocols at the facility and knew exactly how to exploit any weaknesses.

- **The Inside Man**

No heist of this magnitude could be executed without inside help. The Banknote Bonanza involved one or more insiders—employees of the facility who were either coerced, bribed, or ideologically motivated to assist the criminals. These insiders provided crucial information about the layout of the facility, the timing of security shifts, and the location of the most valuable banknotes.

The insiders were carefully chosen for their access to sensitive areas and their ability to operate without raising suspicion. They played a key role in disabling security systems at critical moments, ensuring that the criminals could move through the facility undetected. Their participation was risky, but the rewards promised by the mastermind were too great to resist.

- **The Heist Team**

The heist team was composed of experts in various fields—each member chosen for their specific skills. There were security system hackers, who could bypass alarms and surveillance cameras; logistics experts, who planned the transportation of the stolen banknotes; and muscle, who provided the necessary force to subdue any guards or employees who got in their way.

The team operated with military precision, each member knowing their role and executing it flawlessly. Communication was key, with the team using encrypted channels to coordinate their actions and avoid detection. The heist was planned down to the last detail, with contingency plans in place for any unforeseen complications.

The Execution: A Night of Unprecedented Precision

The execution of the Banknote Bonanza was a masterclass in criminal planning. The heist took place over the course of a single night, during a time when the facility was operating with a reduced staff and security presence. The team had chosen this window carefully, knowing that it offered the best chance of success with the least risk.

- **Step One: Infiltration**

The infiltration of the facility was the first and most critical step in the heist. The team used a combination of forged credentials, insider assistance, and advanced hacking techniques to gain access to the facility. The insiders had already provided the team with key access cards and codes, allowing them to move through the initial security checkpoints without raising alarms.

Once inside, the team split into smaller groups, each with a specific task. The hackers went to work disabling surveillance cameras and motion detectors, creating a virtual blind spot within the facility. Meanwhile, other members of the team moved towards the vaults where the banknotes were stored, using the information provided by the insiders to navigate the complex layout.

- **Step Two: Securing the Loot**

The vaults containing the banknotes were the primary target of the heist. These vaults were equipped with state-of-the-art security, including time-locked doors, biometric scanners, and reinforced steel walls. However, the team had come prepared. Using specialized equipment, they were able to bypass the biometric scanners and override the time-lock mechanisms.

Once inside the vaults, the team quickly set to work loading the banknotes into specially designed containers. These containers were built to be easily transported while also shielding their contents from detection by any security scanners or tracking devices. The amount of cash they were dealing with was staggering—enough to fill several large containers, each worth millions of dollars.

The team worked quickly and efficiently, knowing that time was of the essence. They had planned for this moment meticulously, practicing the operation multiple times to ensure that everything would go smoothly. The containers were loaded onto specially modified vehicles that were waiting in a secure area of the facility.

- **Step Three: The Getaway**

The getaway was arguably the most dangerous part of the heist. The team had to move the stolen banknotes out of the facility and across international borders without being detected. This required not only expert driving but also a carefully planned route that avoided any checkpoints, cameras, or police patrols.

The vehicles used in the getaway were equipped with advanced counter-surveillance technology, allowing the team to evade detection by any security forces that might be on the lookout. The route had been planned to the smallest detail, taking into account traffic patterns, road conditions, and the locations of law enforcement.

Once the team had successfully exited the facility and reached a safe distance, they split up, each taking a different route to their final destination. This was done to minimize the risk of the entire team being captured if one of them was caught. The vehicles were eventually abandoned in a remote location, with the team members continuing on foot or by other means to reach their safe houses.

The Aftermath: A Financial Shockwave

The immediate aftermath of the Banknote Bonanza was chaos. When the facility's morning shift arrived, they found the vaults empty and the security systems compromised. The scale of the heist became apparent almost immediately, and the alarm was raised at the highest levels of government and law enforcement.

- **The Investigation**

The investigation into the Banknote Bonanza was one of the largest and most intensive in history. Law enforcement agencies from multiple countries were involved, including Interpol, as the heist had international implications. The facility itself was thoroughly examined, with every detail of the heist scrutinized in an attempt to identify the perpetrators.

Investigators quickly realized that they were dealing with professionals. The level of sophistication displayed by the criminals was unlike anything they had encountered before. The use of advanced technology, the precise timing, and the insider knowledge all pointed to a highly organized and well-funded criminal operation.

The investigation focused on tracing the stolen banknotes, but this proved to be a monumental challenge. The criminals had taken steps to ensure that the banknotes could not be easily traced, possibly by altering or laundering them through a series of complex financial transactions. The investigation also looked into the possibility of insider involvement, questioning employees and reviewing their backgrounds for any signs of complicity.

- **The Media Frenzy**

The Banknote Bonanza quickly became a global news story, with media outlets covering every twist and turn of the investigation. The public was fascinated by the audacity of the crime and the mystery surrounding the identities of the criminals. The heist was portrayed as a modern-day Robin Hood story, with the criminals seen by some as folk heroes who had outsmarted the financial system.

The media coverage only added to the pressure on law enforcement to solve the case. Every new development was dissected and analyzed, with journalists speculating about the motives and backgrounds of the criminals. The Banknote Bonanza became a cultural phenomenon, inspiring books, documentaries, and even fictionalized accounts.

- **The Financial Impact**

The financial impact of the Banknote Bonanza was significant. The stolen banknotes represented a substantial amount of money, and their sudden disappearance sent shockwaves through the financial system. Banks and financial institutions that relied on the facility for their cash supplies were forced to scramble to make up the shortfall, leading to temporary shortages and disruptions in some areas.

The heist also had broader economic implications. The sheer scale of the theft raised concerns about the security of the global financial system, with some questioning whether other facilities could be vulnerable to similar attacks. Governments and financial regulators began to review and strengthen security measures at other banknote printing facilities and vaults around the world.

In the longer term, the Banknote Bonanza led to changes in the way banknotes were handled and stored. New technologies were developed to make it more difficult for criminals to steal or counterfeit cash, and security protocols were overhauled to prevent a similar heist from happening again.

The Legacy: A Heist That Will Never Be Forgotten

The Banknote Bonanza has gone down in history as one of the most daring and successful heists of all time. The sheer audacity of the crime, the meticulous planning, and the fact that the criminals were able to make off with such a large amount of cash have ensured its place in the annals of criminal legend.

- **The Criminals' Fate**

The fate of the criminals behind the Banknote Bonanza remains a mystery. Despite the best efforts of law enforcement, no one was ever caught or charged in connection with the heist. The criminals managed to disappear without a trace, leaving behind a trail of speculation and unanswered questions.

Some believe that the criminals are still out there, living off the proceeds of the heist in some distant corner of the world. Others think that they may have retired from a life of crime, having pulled off the ultimate score. The possibility that the criminals could strike again has kept law enforcement on high alert, even years after the heist.

- **The Cultural Impact**

The Banknote Bonanza has become a cultural touchstone, inspiring countless works of fiction and non-fiction. The heist has been the subject of books, movies, and television shows, each offering a different interpretation of the crime and the criminals behind it. The story has taken on a life of its own, becoming a symbol of both the dangers and the allure of the criminal underworld.

The heist has also sparked debates about the nature of crime and punishment. Some view the criminals as antiheroes who exposed the vulnerabilities of a corrupt financial system, while others see them as ruthless opportunists who profited at the expense of ordinary people. The Banknote Bonanza has become a case study in criminology, with experts analyzing the heist for insights into the psychology and tactics of high-level criminals.

The Enduring Mystery

The Banknote Bonanza remains an enduring mystery, one that continues to fascinate and intrigue people around the world. The unanswered questions—who were the criminals, how did they pull off the heist, and where is the money now—ensure that the story will be retold for generations to come.

The heist serves as a reminder of the power of human ingenuity and the lengths to which some will go in pursuit of wealth. It also highlights the vulnerabilities of even the most secure systems, showing that no matter how well-guarded, no target is truly safe from those who are determined to take it.

In the end, the Banknote Bonanza is more than just a crime story—it is a reflection of the complexities and contradictions of modern society, where the lines between right and wrong, hero and villain, are often blurred. The legacy of the heist will endure, not just as a tale of criminal daring, but as a symbol of the ever-present tension between order and chaos in the human experience.

Chapter 17: The Ingenious Isabella Stewart Gardner Art Theft

The Isabella Stewart Gardner Museum in Boston, Massachusetts, is renowned for its eclectic collection of priceless works of art, carefully curated by the museum's namesake, Isabella Stewart Gardner. Established in 1903, the museum is housed in a building designed to resemble a 15th-century Venetian palace, reflecting Gardner's deep love for art and culture. Over the years, it has become a cultural landmark, attracting art lovers from around the world to view its impressive array of paintings, sculptures, tapestries, and decorative arts.

However, the museum's illustrious reputation was forever tarnished on the night of March 18, 1990, when it became the scene of one of the most infamous and audacious art thefts in history. In a heist that has captivated the world for over three decades, two men disguised as police officers gained entry to the museum and made off with 13 pieces of art valued at over $500 million. The stolen works included masterpieces by Vermeer, Rembrandt, Degas, and Manet, making it the largest and most significant art theft in history. Despite extensive investigations, the case remains unsolved, and the stolen artworks have never been recovered.

The Isabella Stewart Gardner Museum heist is not just a tale of stolen art; it is a story of intrigue, deception, and the enduring mystery of what happened to the missing masterpieces. The theft has become a symbol of the vulnerability of cultural treasures and the lengths to which some will go to possess them.

The Night of the Heist: A Deceptive Entry

In the early hours of March 18, 1990, as the city of Boston was winding down from St. Patrick's Day celebrations, the Isabella Stewart Gardner

Museum was quiet and secure, or so it seemed. At approximately 1:24 a.m., two men dressed as Boston police officers rang the buzzer at the side entrance of the museum. They informed the security guards on duty, Richard Abath and Randy Hestand, that they were responding to a disturbance call. The guards, inexperienced and unaware of any such call, were caught off guard by the unexpected visit.

Against standard protocol, the guards allowed the men to enter the museum. Abath, who was stationed at the security desk, was the first to greet the "officers." The men asked him to step away from the desk, claiming they needed to confirm his identity. Moments later, one of the men informed Abath that he looked familiar and that there might be an outstanding warrant for his arrest. Abath, confused and compliant, allowed the men to handcuff him. It was then that the realization hit—these were not police officers.

The intruders quickly handcuffed Hestand as well and led both guards to the museum's basement, where they were bound with duct tape and secured to pipes. The men informed the guards that they would not be harmed and left them in the basement, effectively neutralizing the only human element of the museum's security system.

With the guards incapacitated, the thieves had free rein of the museum. They began their heist, methodically moving through the galleries and selecting the artworks they would steal. The entire operation lasted 81 minutes, during which the thieves stole 13 pieces of art, including some of the most valuable and iconic works in the museum's collection.

The Stolen Masterpieces: Irreplaceable Losses

The thieves exhibited a mixture of careful planning and seemingly haphazard decision-making in their selection of the stolen artworks. Among the 13 stolen pieces were several masterpieces that were central to the museum's collection:

1. **"The Concert" by Johannes Vermeer**: One of only 34 known works by the Dutch master, Vermeer's "The Concert" was the most valuable piece stolen during the heist. It depicts three figures around a harpsichord, engaged in a private musical performance. The painting's serene atmosphere and exquisite detail made it a highlight of the museum's collection, and its loss was a devastating blow to the art world.

2. **"The Storm on the Sea of Galilee" by Rembrandt**: This dramatic seascape was Rembrandt's only known seascape painting. It depicts the biblical story of Jesus calming a storm, with the disciples in a state of panic as their boat is battered by the waves. The painting's dynamic composition and emotional intensity made it one of the most admired works in the museum. The thieves cut it from its frame, leaving only the empty wooden frame behind.

3. **"A Lady and Gentleman in Black" by Rembrandt**: Another masterpiece by Rembrandt, this double portrait of a man and woman in formal black attire was also cut from its frame. The painting's rich textures and lifelike depiction of the subjects exemplify Rembrandt's skill in portraiture.

4. **"Landscape with an Obelisk" attributed to Govert Flinck**: Originally attributed to Rembrandt, this painting was later reattributed to his pupil, Govert Flinck. The landscape features a dramatic scene with a towering obelisk, and its theft further added to the mystery surrounding the heist.

5. **"Chez Tortoni" by Édouard Manet**: This small but exquisite portrait by the French Impressionist Manet depicts a man seated at a café table, casually sketching on a sheet of paper. The painting's intimate scale and lively brushwork made it a favorite among visitors.

6. **Five Works on Paper by Edgar Degas**: The thieves also stole five sketches by the French artist Edgar Degas, known for his

depictions of ballet dancers and scenes of Parisian life. These works included "Cortege aux Environs de Florence," "La Sortie de Pesage," "Program for an Artistic Soiree 1," "Program for an Artistic Soiree 2," and "Three Mounted Jockeys." The sketches, though smaller and less valuable than the other stolen pieces, were significant examples of Degas's mastery of movement and composition.

7. **A Chinese Ku (Bronze Vessel)**: In addition to the paintings, the thieves also took a 12th-century Chinese bronze vessel known as a "Ku." This ancient artifact, used for rituals and ceremonies, was a unique and valuable piece in the museum's collection.

8. **A Finial from a Napoleonic Flag**: The thieves also removed a small finial, or decorative ornament, from a Napoleonic flag in the museum's collection. The finial's theft was puzzling, as it held little monetary value compared to the other stolen items.

The stolen works represented a wide range of artistic styles and periods, from Dutch Golden Age painting to French Impressionism, and their loss left a significant void in the museum's collection. The thieves appeared to have a specific plan in mind, bypassing many other valuable works in the museum and focusing on these particular pieces. However, their selection also raised questions—why did they take certain items while leaving others behind?

The Investigation: A Search for Answers

The morning after the heist, museum staff arrived to find the museum in disarray. The empty frames, cut from their canvases, hung on the walls as haunting reminders of the stolen masterpieces. The guards were found still tied up in the basement, unharmed but shaken. The museum immediately alerted the authorities, and the FBI launched an investigation into the theft.

The initial investigation faced several challenges. The thieves had been careful not to leave behind any significant evidence—no fingerprints, no DNA, and no security footage that could identify them. The museum's security system, though equipped with motion detectors, was outdated and provided little useful information. The thieves had avoided the motion detectors in certain areas, suggesting they had knowledge of the museum's layout and security measures.

The investigation quickly expanded to include art experts, criminologists, and international law enforcement agencies. The FBI explored several leads, including the possibility that the theft was orchestrated by organized crime groups. Boston, at the time, was home to several notorious crime families, and some investigators believed that the stolen art may have been used as collateral in illicit dealings.

One of the most promising leads came from a tipster who claimed to have information about the whereabouts of the stolen art. The tipster provided details that led investigators to several locations in Boston and surrounding areas, but each search proved fruitless. The stolen artworks remained elusive, and the trail gradually grew cold.

Over the years, the FBI has offered a reward of up to $10 million for information leading to the recovery of the stolen art, making it one of the largest rewards ever offered by the agency. Despite this, the case remains unsolved, and the stolen works have yet to resurface.

Theories and Speculation: Who Were the Thieves?

The mystery of who carried out the Isabella Stewart Gardner Museum heist has spawned numerous theories and speculation. Some of the most prominent theories include:

1. **The Local Criminals Theory**: One theory suggests that the heist was carried out by local criminals with connections to

Boston's organized crime scene. The thieves' knowledge of the museum's security system and their ability to avoid detection suggest that they may have had inside information. Some investigators believe that the stolen art was hidden or sold within the local criminal underworld.

2. **The International Art Theft Ring Theory**: Another theory posits that the theft was part of a larger operation by an international art theft ring. The thieves may have been hired by a wealthy collector or criminal organization to steal specific works of art. According to this theory, the stolen art may have been smuggled out of the country and sold on the black market.

3. **The Inside Job Theory**: Some have speculated that the theft may have been an inside job, involving someone with intimate knowledge of the museum's security systems and procedures. This theory suggests that the thieves had assistance from someone within the museum or from a former employee.

4. **The Whitey Bulger Connection**: James "Whitey" Bulger, the notorious Boston crime boss, has also been linked to the heist in some theories. Bulger's criminal empire was at its peak during the time of the theft, and some believe that he may have been involved in orchestrating or facilitating the heist. However, no concrete evidence has ever surfaced to support this theory.

5. **The False Flag Theory**: A more unconventional theory suggests that the heist may have been a "false flag" operation, intended to distract law enforcement from other criminal activities. According to this theory, the theft was carried out to create chaos and divert attention from other crimes taking place in Boston at the time.

Despite the numerous theories, none have been definitively proven, and the identities of the thieves remain unknown. The lack of arrests and the absence of the stolen art have only deepened the mystery, leaving investigators and the public to wonder who could have pulled off such a daring and sophisticated heist.

The Impact on the Art World: A Void That Cannot Be Filled

The Isabella Stewart Gardner Museum heist had a profound impact on the art world, both in terms of the loss of the stolen works and the broader implications for art security. The theft of 13 priceless pieces of art, including masterpieces by some of the most revered artists in history, was a devastating blow to the cultural heritage of Boston and the world.

The loss of "The Concert" by Vermeer, in particular, was a significant cultural tragedy. Vermeer's work is rare, with only a few dozen paintings attributed to him, and "The Concert" was one of his finest. Its absence has left a void in the understanding and appreciation of Vermeer's contribution to art history.

Similarly, the loss of Rembrandt's "The Storm on the Sea of Galilee" and "A Lady and Gentleman in Black" deprived the public of the opportunity to experience the genius of one of the greatest painters of all time. Rembrandt's work is celebrated for its emotional depth and technical mastery, and the theft of these paintings was a significant loss to the art world.

The heist also highlighted the vulnerability of museums and cultural institutions to theft. The Isabella Stewart Gardner Museum, like many other museums, was not equipped with the advanced security systems that are now standard in the industry. The theft exposed weaknesses in the museum's security protocols and prompted many institutions to reevaluate their own security measures.

In the years following the heist, museums around the world implemented stricter security protocols, including the installation of more sophisticated alarm systems, surveillance cameras, and motion detectors. The theft also led to increased collaboration between museums, law enforcement agencies, and international organizations to combat art theft and recover stolen works.

The Aftermath: A Museum in Mourning

In the wake of the heist, the Isabella Stewart Gardner Museum was left to grapple with the loss of its most treasured pieces. The empty frames that once held the stolen paintings remain on display in the museum's galleries, a poignant reminder of what was lost. Isabella Stewart Gardner's will stipulated that the arrangement of the museum's collection should remain unchanged, and the museum has honored this wish by leaving the empty frames in place.

The museum has continued to thrive despite the loss, drawing visitors from around the world who come to experience the remaining collection and learn about the history of the heist. The theft has become an integral part of the museum's story, and the ongoing search for the stolen art has kept the public's interest alive.

In recent years, the museum has also taken steps to engage the public in the search for the stolen art. The museum's website features a section dedicated to the heist, providing information about the stolen works and encouraging anyone with information to come forward. The museum has also hosted events and exhibitions related to the theft, further raising awareness of the missing masterpieces.

The Legacy of the Heist: An Unsolved Mystery

The Isabella Stewart Gardner Museum heist remains one of the greatest unsolved mysteries in the art world. Despite decades of investigation, the identities of the thieves and the whereabouts of the stolen art remain unknown. The case continues to captivate the public and inspire new theories, documentaries, books, and even fictionalized accounts of the heist.

The theft has become a symbol of the enduring allure of art and the lengths to which people will go to possess it. It has also raised important questions about the responsibility of museums and cultural institutions to protect their collections and the challenges of recovering stolen art.

As the years go by, the hope of recovering the stolen works may seem increasingly remote, but the search continues. The FBI has not closed the case, and the museum remains committed to finding the missing pieces and restoring them to their rightful place. The reward for information leading to the recovery of the stolen art remains one of the largest ever offered, a testament to the value and significance of the missing works.

Conclusion: The Enduring Mystery

The Isabella Stewart Gardner Museum heist is a story of intrigue, deception, and loss. It is a reminder of the fragility of cultural heritage and the enduring mystery of the missing masterpieces. As long as the stolen art remains unrecovered, the heist will continue to captivate the imagination and inspire those who seek to solve one of the greatest mysteries in the history of art. The empty frames in the museum's galleries stand as a silent testament to what was lost, and the search for the stolen art remains a quest that is far from over.

Chapter 18: The Secrets of the Stolen Stradivarius

In the world of classical music, few names command as much reverence and mystique as Antonio Stradivari, the master luthier whose violins have become synonymous with perfection in craftsmanship and sound. Stradivari, who lived from 1644 to 1737 in Cremona, Italy, created instruments that are considered the pinnacle of string instrument construction. His violins, known as Stradivarius, are celebrated for their unparalleled tonal quality, clarity, and power. Over the centuries, these violins have been played by some of the greatest musicians in history, and they remain the most sought-after instruments by collectors, musicians, and enthusiasts alike.

The allure of a Stradivarius violin is not only due to its exceptional sound but also its rarity. Of the approximately 1,100 instruments Stradivari crafted during his lifetime, around 650 survive today, and many of these are in the hands of museums, collectors, or professional musicians. The scarcity of Stradivarius violins, combined with their extraordinary value—some are worth millions of dollars—has made them the target of numerous thefts and heists over the years. Each theft of a Stradivarius violin is a story unto itself, filled with intrigue, deception, and, in some cases, mystery that remains unsolved to this day.

The thefts of Stradivarius violins often transcend the typical bounds of criminal activity, entering into the realm of legend. These stolen instruments are not mere objects; they are considered priceless works of art, imbued with a history and cultural significance that elevates them above the ordinary. The secrecy surrounding these thefts only adds to their allure, as each stolen Stradivarius becomes the subject of speculation, rumor, and sometimes even conspiracy theories. The stories of these thefts are a testament to the enduring fascination with Stradivarius violins and the lengths to which people will go to possess them.

This exploration of the secrets of the stolen Stradivarius delves into the history of these legendary instruments, the reasons behind their extraordinary value, and the most infamous thefts that have occurred over the centuries. It is a story of art, crime, and the human desire to possess something truly extraordinary, even if it means breaking the law.

Antonio Stradivari and the Creation of a Legend

To understand the significance of a stolen Stradivarius, one must first appreciate the genius of Antonio Stradivari, the man behind these legendary instruments. Born in 1644 in Cremona, Italy, Stradivari was part of a tradition of violin making that had been established in the city by earlier luthiers such as Andrea Amati. Stradivari apprenticed under Niccolò Amati, Andrea's grandson, and it was under his tutelage that Stradivari honed his craft and began to develop his own unique approach to violin making.

Stradivari's violins are renowned for their exceptional craftsmanship, attention to detail, and innovative design. He experimented with the dimensions of the violin, altering the shape, size, and thickness of the body to achieve a sound that was both powerful and refined. Stradivari also developed a unique varnish, the composition of which remains a closely guarded secret to this day. This varnish not only contributed to the visual beauty of the instruments but also played a crucial role in enhancing their tonal qualities.

The period between 1700 and 1720 is often referred to as Stradivari's "Golden Period," during which he created some of his most famous and valuable instruments. These violins are characterized by their rich, warm sound, which has been described as having a "singing" quality. The violins from this period, such as the "Viotti" and the "Messiah," are considered masterpieces and are among the most coveted Stradivarius instruments in existence.

Stradivari's reputation as the greatest violin maker of all time was solidified during his lifetime, and his instruments quickly became the standard by which all others were judged. Over the centuries, Stradivarius violins have been played by some of the most celebrated musicians in history, including Niccolò Paganini, Itzhak Perlman, and Yehudi Menuhin. The instruments' association with such illustrious figures has only added to their mystique and value.

The rarity of Stradivarius violins, combined with their extraordinary sound, has made them highly sought after by collectors and musicians alike. As a result, these instruments have become targets for thieves who seek to profit from their immense value. The thefts of Stradivarius violins are not just crimes of opportunity; they are often meticulously planned heists that require a deep understanding of the instrument's history, provenance, and significance.

The Intrigue of Stradivarius Thefts: Why Steal a Stradivarius?

The theft of a Stradivarius violin is not a simple act of larceny; it is a crime that involves considerable risk, planning, and knowledge. The reasons behind these thefts are as varied as the individuals who commit them, but they all share a common motivation: the desire to possess or profit from one of the most valuable and revered objects in the world.

One of the primary motivations for stealing a Stradivarius is its immense monetary value. Stradivarius violins are among the most expensive musical instruments in the world, with some selling for tens of millions of dollars. The rarity of these instruments, combined with their historical significance and association with legendary musicians, has driven their prices to astronomical levels. For thieves, the prospect of selling a stolen Stradivarius on the black market or to a private collector can be an irresistible temptation.

However, stealing a Stradivarius for monetary gain is fraught with challenges. The high-profile nature of these instruments makes them difficult to sell without attracting attention. Stradivarius violins are well-documented, and their provenance is often meticulously recorded, making it difficult for a thief to sell the instrument without raising suspicion. Furthermore, the small, tight-knit community of violin experts and dealers is highly vigilant, and any attempt to sell a stolen Stradivarius is likely to be quickly noticed.

In some cases, the theft of a Stradivarius may be motivated by a desire for prestige or personal satisfaction. Possessing a Stradivarius, even illegally, can confer a sense of power and status. The idea of owning one of the most famous and valuable violins in the world, even if it must be hidden away from public view, can be a powerful incentive for certain individuals. For some thieves, the act of stealing a Stradivarius is as much about the thrill of the heist as it is about the potential financial reward.

There are also instances where the theft of a Stradivarius is driven by a deep appreciation for the instrument itself. Some thieves are musicians or collectors who have a profound love for the violin and a desire to possess a Stradivarius, regardless of the legal or ethical implications. These individuals may justify their actions by believing that they are "rescuing" the instrument from a neglectful owner or that they can care for it better than its rightful owner.

Regardless of the motivation, the theft of a Stradivarius is always a high-stakes crime that carries significant legal and personal risks. The stories of these thefts are often filled with drama, deception, and, in some cases, tragic outcomes. The following sections explore some of the most infamous Stradivarius thefts in history, each of which reveals the unique challenges and mysteries associated with stealing one of the world's most prized instruments.

The Infamous Thefts: A History of Stolen Stradivarius Violins

Throughout history, numerous Stradivarius violins have been stolen, each case shrouded in its own unique set of circumstances, intrigue, and, sometimes, resolution. The following are some of the most notorious Stradivarius thefts, each illustrating the lengths to which thieves will go to obtain these priceless instruments.

- **The Theft of the "Davidoff-Morini" Stradivarius (1995)**

One of the most mysterious and unresolved Stradivarius thefts occurred in 1995 when the "Davidoff-Morini" Stradivarius, a violin made in 1727, was stolen from the New York City apartment of renowned violinist Erica Morini. The theft took place shortly before Morini's death at the age of 91, and the circumstances surrounding the crime have remained a subject of speculation and intrigue.

Erica Morini was one of the most celebrated violinists of the 20th century, known for her extraordinary skill and emotional depth. The "Davidoff-Morini" Stradivarius was her prized possession, an instrument she had played throughout her illustrious career. The violin, named after its previous owners, was valued at several million dollars at the time of the theft.

The details of the theft are murky. Morini's apartment was not forcibly entered, leading some to speculate that the thief was someone she knew or trusted. The violin was taken along with several other valuable items, but it was clear that the Stradivarius was the primary target. Despite extensive investigations by law enforcement and private detectives, the

"Davidoff-Morini" Stradivarius has never been recovered, and the identity of the thief remains unknown.

The theft of the "Davidoff-Morini" Stradivarius is particularly poignant because it occurred at the end of Morini's life, depriving her of the instrument she had cherished and played for decades. The violin's disappearance has left a void in the world of classical music, and its whereabouts continue to be a subject of speculation among violin experts and enthusiasts.

- **The Robbery of the "Lipinski" Stradivarius (2014)**

In 2014, the "Lipinski" Stradivarius, a violin made in 1715, was stolen in a brazen armed robbery in Milwaukee, Wisconsin. The violin was in the possession of concertmaster Frank Almond, who was attacked with a stun gun by two assailants as he was leaving a performance. The thieves made off with the violin, which was valued at over $5 million.

The "Lipinski" Stradivarius has a storied history, having been owned by some of the most prominent musicians in history, including Giuseppe Tartini and Karol Lipinski, after whom it is named. The violin's theft was a shocking and audacious crime, carried out with a level of planning and sophistication that suggested the involvement of individuals with knowledge of the instrument's value and significance.

The robbery sparked a massive investigation, with law enforcement agencies working tirelessly to recover the violin. The case drew international attention, with experts and musicians expressing concern that the "Lipinski" Stradivarius might never be seen again. However, unlike many other Stradivarius thefts, this story had a happy ending. The violin was recovered nine days after the robbery, hidden in the attic of one of the thieves' associates. The perpetrators were apprehended and sentenced to prison, and the "Lipinski" Stradivarius was returned to its rightful owner.

The recovery of the "Lipinski" Stradivarius was a rare and fortunate outcome, highlighting the challenges of stealing and attempting to sell such a well-known and valuable instrument. The case also underscored the lengths to which law enforcement and the musical community will go to protect and recover these priceless violins.

- **The Heist of the "Kreutzer" Stradivarius (1998)**

Another notable Stradivarius theft occurred in 1998 when the "Kreutzer" Stradivarius, made in 1727, was stolen from the Ealing home of virtuoso violinist Peter Shah, in London. The violin, named after the French violinist Rodolphe Kreutzer, was taken along with two bows, valued at £50,000 each, and a Guadagnini violin. The total value of the stolen items was estimated at over £1 million.

The theft was a devastating blow to Shah, who had spent years performing with the "Kreutzer" Stradivarius. The violin was insured for £900,000, but its loss was felt far more keenly on a personal and professional level. Despite efforts to recover the instrument, the "Kreutzer" Stradivarius has never been found, and its fate remains a mystery.

The theft of the "Kreutzer" Stradivarius highlights the vulnerability of even the most cherished and well-protected instruments. For musicians like Shah, the loss of a Stradivarius is not just a financial loss; it is the loss of a lifelong companion, an instrument that has become an extension of the artist's own voice.

- **The Disappearance of the "Gibson" Stradivarius (1936)**

One of the earliest and most enduring mysteries in the history of Stradivarius thefts is the disappearance of the "Gibson" Stradivarius in 1936. The violin, made in 1713, was stolen from the London home of renowned violinist Bronisław Huberman during a concert at Carnegie

Hall. The theft was audacious, as the violin was taken while Huberman was performing on stage with a different instrument.

The "Gibson" Stradivarius was not immediately missed, as Huberman was unaware that it had been stolen until after the concert. The violin's disappearance remained a mystery for nearly 50 years, during which time it was believed to be lost forever. However, in 1985, the violin resurfaced under extraordinary circumstances.

A violinist named Julian Altman, who had been playing the instrument for decades, confessed to his wife on his deathbed that the violin he had been using was, in fact, the stolen "Gibson" Stradivarius. Altman had acquired the violin shortly after the theft and had managed to keep it hidden for nearly half a century. After his confession, the violin was authenticated and returned to its rightful owner.

The story of the "Gibson" Stradivarius is a testament to the enduring nature of these instruments and the lengths to which people will go to possess them. The violin's eventual recovery after so many years is a rare and remarkable outcome in the world of stolen Stradivarius violins, where many remain lost to history.

The Challenges of Recovering Stolen Stradivarius Violins

Recovering a stolen Stradivarius violin is an extraordinarily difficult task, even with the resources and expertise available to law enforcement agencies and private investigators. The challenges associated with recovering these instruments are numerous, and they stem from the very qualities that make Stradivarius violins so valuable: their rarity, uniqueness, and historical significance.

One of the primary challenges in recovering a stolen Stradivarius is the difficulty in selling the instrument. Due to their rarity and the extensive documentation that often accompanies them, Stradivarius violins are well-known to experts, dealers, and musicians. Any attempt to sell a stolen Stradivarius is likely to raise red flags, as the instrument's provenance will be closely scrutinized. The tight-knit nature of the violin community further complicates matters for thieves, as news of a stolen Stradivarius spreads quickly, making it nearly impossible to sell the instrument without being detected.

Another challenge is the potential for the instrument to be hidden away for years, or even decades, as was the case with the "Gibson" Stradivarius. Thieves may choose to keep the violin rather than risk selling it, either for personal use or simply to hold onto a piece of history. In such cases, the instrument may remain out of sight for a long time, with its whereabouts unknown to the world. This creates a situation where the violin may never be recovered, or it may only resurface many years later under unusual circumstances.

The delicate nature of Stradivarius violins also poses a challenge in recovery efforts. These instruments are fragile and require careful handling and maintenance. If a stolen Stradivarius is not properly cared for, it may suffer damage that diminishes its value and sound quality. In some cases, thieves may not have the expertise to care for the instrument, leading to irreversible harm. This adds a sense of urgency to recovery efforts, as the longer the violin remains in the wrong hands, the greater the risk of damage.

The global nature of the art and antiquities market further complicates recovery efforts. Stolen Stradivarius violins can be transported across borders and sold in international markets, making it difficult for law enforcement to track their movements. The involvement of unscrupulous dealers, collectors, or intermediaries who are willing to facilitate the sale of a stolen Stradivarius adds another layer of complexity to the recovery process.

Despite these challenges, there have been successes in recovering stolen Stradivarius violins, thanks to the dedication and persistence of law enforcement agencies, private investigators, and the global violin community. The recovery of the "Lipinski" Stradivarius in 2014 is a prime example of how a combination of modern investigative techniques, community vigilance, and a bit of luck can lead to the return of a priceless instrument.

The Enduring Mystique of Stradivarius Violins

The thefts of Stradivarius violins are not just crimes; they are stories that capture the imagination and highlight the enduring mystique of these extraordinary instruments. Each stolen Stradivarius carries with it a sense of history, artistry, and cultural significance that elevates it above mere monetary value. The desire to possess a Stradivarius, even through illicit means, speaks to the deep emotional and artistic connection that these violins inspire.

The stories of stolen Stradivarius violins also underscore the broader human fascination with rarity, beauty, and the unattainable. The allure of a Stradivarius is not just in its sound or craftsmanship, but in its status as an object of desire that represents the pinnacle of artistic achievement. For those who seek to steal a Stradivarius, the act is often driven by a combination of greed, admiration, and the thrill of acquiring something truly exceptional.

The secrecy and intrigue that surround Stradivarius thefts only add to the mystique of these instruments. The unknown fates of many stolen Stradivarius violins create a sense of mystery that continues to captivate collectors, musicians, and the public. Each missing Stradivarius becomes a ghost story of sorts, a tale of a lost masterpiece that may one day resurface under surprising circumstances.

In the end, the secrets of the stolen Stradivarius are as much about the violins themselves as they are about the people who seek to possess them. These stories remind us of the power of art to inspire both beauty and obsession, and they highlight the enduring appeal of objects that transcend time, culture, and even legality.

The legacy of the Stradivarius violins, including those that have been stolen, is one of timeless artistry and enduring fascination. As long as these instruments continue to exist, so too will the stories of their thefts, recoveries, and the mysteries that surround them.

Chapter 19: The Great Whiskey Warehouse Robbery

Whiskey, often referred to as "liquid gold," has been a cherished spirit for centuries, enjoyed by connoisseurs, collectors, and casual drinkers alike. Its production is an art form, requiring precise methods, quality ingredients, and, most importantly, time. Aged in oak barrels, whiskey develops complex flavors that make it one of the most sought-after spirits in the world. Its value increases with age and rarity, and certain bottles can fetch thousands, even hundreds of thousands, of dollars at auction.

The allure of whiskey goes beyond its taste; it carries cultural, historical, and even spiritual significance. In countries like Scotland, Ireland, and the United States, whiskey is more than just a drink—it's a symbol of heritage and tradition. The careful crafting of whiskey, passed down through generations, gives it a unique place in the hearts of those who produce and consume it.

Given its high value, both in monetary terms and cultural significance, whiskey has often been the target of theft. The most audacious of these thefts was the Great Whiskey Warehouse Robbery, a crime that stunned the industry and captivated the public. This heist, which unfolded over a period of time, involved not only the theft of valuable barrels of whiskey but also a complex web of deceit, conspiracy, and eventual downfall.

The Setting: The Rise of the Bourbon Industry

To understand the significance of the Great Whiskey Warehouse Robbery, it's important to delve into the history and growth of the bourbon industry in the United States. Bourbon, a distinctly American form of whiskey, has its roots in the late 18th century when settlers in Kentucky began distilling surplus corn into whiskey. The rich, limestone-filtered water in the region, combined with the fertile soil, made Kentucky the perfect place for producing high-quality bourbon.

By the 19th century, bourbon had become a staple of American culture, with numerous distilleries operating throughout Kentucky and other states. The spirit was aged in charred oak barrels, which gave it a distinctive flavor profile characterized by notes of caramel, vanilla, and oak. Over time, certain brands and distilleries gained reputations for producing exceptional bourbon, and some bottles became highly coveted.

The 20th century saw both challenges and opportunities for the bourbon industry. Prohibition in the United States (1920-1933) nearly destroyed the industry, but a few distilleries managed to survive by producing "medicinal" whiskey, which was legally allowed during the dry years. After Prohibition was repealed, the bourbon industry slowly recovered, and by the late 20th and early 21st centuries, it was thriving once again, with a renewed interest in aged and rare whiskeys.

As bourbon grew in popularity, so did the value of older, rarer bottles. Collectors and enthusiasts began to seek out limited-edition releases and vintage bottles, some of which were decades old. The demand for high-quality bourbon led to skyrocketing prices, making it a lucrative target for theft.

The Players: The Warehouse and the Workers

The stage for the Great Whiskey Warehouse Robbery was set in the heart of Kentucky's bourbon country, where some of the most famous distilleries in the world are located. The warehouses where bourbon is aged are massive structures, often several stories high, with rows upon rows of oak barrels stacked inside. These warehouses, sometimes referred to as "rickhouses," are where the magic happens, as the whiskey ages and develops its signature flavors.

The workers at these distilleries and warehouses are often lifelong employees, many of whom have deep ties to the industry. These men and women are entrusted with the care of millions of dollars' worth of bourbon, overseeing everything from the distillation process to the aging and bottling of the final product. They are the guardians of a tradition that has been passed down for generations, and their role is crucial in maintaining the quality and integrity of the bourbon produced.

However, the high value of the whiskey stored in these warehouses also makes them tempting targets for theft. The barrels inside are often worth thousands of dollars each, and as the whiskey ages, its value only increases. For some workers, the temptation to pilfer a barrel or two—especially when faced with financial difficulties or the allure of quick money—can be too great to resist.

This was the case in the Great Whiskey Warehouse Robbery, where a group of insiders, including warehouse workers and accomplices, conspired to steal and sell barrels of bourbon over a period of time. Their actions would not only result in one of the most notorious whiskey heists in history but also expose vulnerabilities in the industry and lead to significant changes in how whiskey is stored and protected.

The Heist: How the Great Whiskey Warehouse Robbery Unfolded

The Great Whiskey Warehouse Robbery wasn't a single event but rather a series of thefts that took place over several years, involving multiple people and a complex operation. The mastermind behind the heist was a warehouse worker with intimate knowledge of the facility and its security—or lack thereof. This insider access allowed the thieves to carefully plan their activities, taking advantage of the lax oversight and the sheer volume of whiskey stored in the warehouse.

The plan was simple yet effective: over time, the thieves would remove barrels of bourbon from the warehouse, replacing them with empty or less valuable barrels to avoid detection. The stolen barrels would then be sold on the black market or to private collectors who were willing to pay a premium for rare, aged bourbon. The thieves were careful not to draw attention to their activities, stealing only a few barrels at a time and ensuring that the losses would go unnoticed in the vast inventory of the warehouse.

The operation was so successful that it continued for years without arousing suspicion. The thieves became more confident and brazen, expanding their activities to include other distilleries and warehouses. At the height of the operation, they were stealing and selling barrels worth hundreds of thousands of dollars, reaping huge profits from their illicit activities.

However, as with many criminal enterprises, greed and overconfidence eventually led to their downfall. The sheer volume of stolen whiskey and the growing rumors within the industry about missing barrels and suspicious sales began to attract attention. Investigators, both private and from law enforcement, started to piece together the clues, and it wasn't long before the net began to close in on the thieves.

The Investigation: Unraveling the Conspiracy

The investigation into the Great Whiskey Warehouse Robbery was a complex and painstaking process, involving multiple agencies and extensive undercover work. Law enforcement officers, including members of the Kentucky State Police and the Bureau of Alcohol, Tobacco, Firearms, and Explosives (ATF), were brought in to track down the stolen whiskey and identify those responsible for the thefts.

One of the key challenges in the investigation was the secretive nature of the whiskey black market. The buyers and sellers of stolen bourbon operated in a shadowy world where transactions were conducted discreetly, often through intermediaries who knew how to cover their tracks. The investigators had to infiltrate this underground network, gaining the trust of those involved while gathering evidence that could lead to arrests and recoveries.

As the investigation progressed, law enforcement officials began to focus on certain individuals who had access to the warehouses and the means to carry out the thefts. Through a combination of surveillance, wiretaps, and undercover operations, they were able to gather enough evidence to make arrests. The breakthrough came when a key member of the theft ring was apprehended and agreed to cooperate with authorities in exchange for a reduced sentence.

With this insider information, investigators were able to unravel the full extent of the conspiracy. They discovered that the thefts had been going on for years, involving not just barrels of bourbon but also bottles of rare and expensive whiskey. The stolen whiskey had been sold to collectors and even bars, some of which unknowingly purchased the illicit product.

The arrests that followed were a major blow to the whiskey theft ring, but they also sent shockwaves through the bourbon industry. The scale of the thefts and the involvement of insiders highlighted serious vulnerabilities in the way whiskey was stored and monitored, leading to calls for stricter security measures and better oversight.

The Aftermath: Legal Repercussions and Industry Reforms

The legal repercussions of the Great Whiskey Warehouse Robbery were significant, with several individuals facing serious charges including theft, conspiracy, and trafficking in stolen goods. Those who were convicted received lengthy prison sentences, reflecting the seriousness of their crimes and the value of the stolen whiskey.

The case also had a lasting impact on the bourbon industry, prompting distilleries and warehouses to reevaluate their security practices. The revelations of how easily the thieves had been able to steal barrels of whiskey led to a renewed focus on preventing such thefts in the future. Many distilleries implemented stricter inventory controls, better tracking systems for barrels, and enhanced security measures including surveillance cameras and increased oversight of warehouse operations.

The Great Whiskey Warehouse Robbery also served as a cautionary tale for the whiskey community, highlighting the risks and challenges of maintaining the integrity of such a valuable product. The case became a topic of discussion at industry conferences and meetings, where experts shared insights and strategies for protecting whiskey from theft.

The incident also had an unintended effect on the market for rare and aged bourbon. The publicity surrounding the thefts and the subsequent recovery of some of the stolen whiskey drew attention to the value and rarity of older bourbon, leading to increased demand and even higher prices for certain bottles. In a sense, the heist inadvertently fueled the very market that had made the thefts so lucrative in the first place.

Legacy: The Great Whiskey Warehouse Robbery in Popular Culture

The Great Whiskey Warehouse Robbery has since become a part of bourbon lore, a story that is recounted with a mix of fascination and disbelief by those in the industry and beyond. The audacity of the thieves, the scale of the thefts, and the drama of the investigation have all contributed to the enduring appeal of the case.

The heist has been the subject of numerous articles, documentaries, and even books, each exploring different aspects of the crime and its impact on the bourbon world. It has also inspired fictional accounts, with authors and filmmakers using the story as a basis for thrillers and crime dramas set in the world of whiskey production.

In popular culture, the Great Whiskey Warehouse Robbery has come to symbolize the lengths to which people will go to obtain a piece of liquid history. It serves as a reminder of the high stakes involved in the production and sale of rare whiskey, and the ever-present temptation that such valuable commodities can present.

Conclusion: A Crime of Opportunity and Obsession

The Great Whiskey Warehouse Robbery was a crime born out of opportunity, insider knowledge, and a deep understanding of the value of the product at the center of the heist. It was a sophisticated operation that exploited weaknesses in the system and took advantage of the growing demand for rare and aged bourbon. The fallout from the robbery was felt throughout the industry, leading to changes in how whiskey is stored and protected.

But beyond the specifics of the crime, the Great Whiskey Warehouse Robbery also taps into a broader narrative about human obsession, greed, and the allure of something precious. In the end, the story is as much about the people who carried out the thefts as it is about the whiskey they stole—a tale of ambition, temptation, and ultimately, the consequences of crossing the line in the pursuit of wealth and status.

The legacy of the Great Whiskey Warehouse Robbery lives on, not just in the changes it brought to the bourbon industry, but in the way it continues to capture the imagination of those who hear the story. It remains one of the most infamous and intriguing crimes in the history of whiskey, a testament to the enduring power of "liquid gold" and the lengths to which people will go to possess it.

Chapter 20: The Case of the Vanished Vermeer

The story of the stolen Johannes Vermeer painting, often referred to as "The Case of the Vanished Vermeer," is one of the most captivating and enduring mysteries in the world of art theft. This case not only highlights the value of Vermeer's work but also reveals the complex web of intrigue, crime, and high-stakes negotiations that surround the theft of priceless cultural treasures.

Johannes Vermeer: The Master of Light and Shadow

Johannes Vermeer, a Dutch painter from the 17th century, is celebrated for his mastery of light, color, and composition. Though his body of work is relatively small—only about 34 paintings are attributed to him—Vermeer's paintings are highly valued for their serene beauty and meticulous attention to detail. His works, such as "The Girl with a Pearl Earring" and "The Milkmaid," have become iconic, representing the pinnacle of Dutch Golden Age painting. Vermeer's ability to capture the subtleties of light and the quiet intimacy of everyday life has made his paintings some of the most sought-after in the art world.

The Heist: A Bold and Brazen Act

The Case of the Vanished Vermeer centers around the infamous theft of one of Vermeer's masterpieces. On the night of March 18, 1990, two men dressed as police officers entered the Isabella Stewart Gardner Museum in Boston, claiming to be responding to a disturbance. Once inside, they overpowered the security guards and proceeded to steal 13 pieces of art, including Vermeer's "The Concert." The thieves worked methodically, cutting the paintings from their frames, and within 81 minutes, they had disappeared into the night, leaving behind an empty frame where "The Concert" once hung.

This heist is considered the largest art theft in history, with the stolen works estimated to be worth over $500 million. Vermeer's "The Concert" alone was valued at around $250 million, making it one of the most valuable missing paintings in the world. The audacity of the crime, coupled with the high value of the stolen art, immediately placed the case in the international spotlight.

The Investigation: A Trail Gone Cold

The investigation into the theft began immediately, but despite the efforts of the FBI, Interpol, and private investigators, the case quickly went cold. The thieves left few clues, and the museum's security system at the time was rudimentary, providing little evidence for authorities to work with. Over the years, numerous theories emerged about the whereabouts of the stolen art and the identity of the thieves.

Some speculated that the theft was the work of organized crime, while others believed it was a high-stakes heist conducted by professional art thieves. Theories also surfaced that the paintings were stolen to be used as collateral in criminal transactions or as leverage in negotiations with law enforcement. Despite these theories, no arrests were made, and the art remained missing.

The Search for "The Concert": A Global Hunt

Vermeer's "The Concert" became a symbol of the lost treasures of the Gardner Museum heist. Investigators and art lovers alike were captivated by the mystery surrounding the painting's disappearance. Over the years, tips and rumors surfaced, leading investigators to search locations across the globe, from warehouses in Boston to the estates of international crime figures.

One of the most promising leads came in 2010 when the FBI announced that they had identified the thieves responsible for the heist. However, the identities of the thieves were never publicly disclosed, and the whereabouts of the stolen art remained unknown. The FBI's announcement renewed hope that the paintings might still be recovered, but it also raised new questions about why the art had not yet been found.

The Legacy of the Vanished Vermeer

The Case of the Vanished Vermeer continues to haunt the art world. The theft not only deprived the public of the opportunity to experience one of Vermeer's masterpieces, but it also highlighted the vulnerability of cultural institutions and the lengths to which criminals will go to profit from art.

The empty frames still hang in the Isabella Stewart Gardner Museum as a poignant reminder of what was lost. The museum has offered a $10 million reward for information leading to the recovery of the stolen art, and the case remains open. Despite the passage of time, the hope of recovering Vermeer's "The Concert" and the other stolen works persists.

The legacy of this heist has also influenced art security measures around the world. Museums and galleries have invested heavily in advanced security systems, and international cooperation in tracking and recovering stolen art has improved significantly. Yet, despite these advancements, the mystery of the vanished Vermeer remains unsolved, a testament to the enduring allure and elusiveness of art.

The Cultural Impact: A Symbol of Loss and Resilience

Beyond the financial value, the theft of Vermeer's "The Concert" represents a significant cultural loss. Vermeer's paintings are rare and irreplaceable, and their theft is a blow not only to the art world but also to humanity's shared cultural heritage. The loss of such a masterpiece is felt deeply by those who appreciate art, history, and the beauty of Vermeer's work.

However, the case also symbolizes resilience and the enduring hope of recovery. The continued efforts to locate the stolen art demonstrate a commitment to preserving and protecting cultural treasures. The art community's refusal to let the memory of the stolen paintings fade away serves as a reminder of the importance of art in our lives and the lengths to which we will go to recover what has been lost.

Modern Efforts and the Ongoing Mystery

In recent years, advancements in technology and forensic analysis have provided new tools for investigators. Digital databases of stolen art, improved communication between law enforcement agencies, and the use of social media to raise public awareness have all played a role in keeping the case alive. Nevertheless, the whereabouts of Vermeer's "The Concert" remain unknown, and the painting continues to be listed as one of the top ten most wanted works of art by the FBI.

The mystery of the vanished Vermeer has also inspired numerous books, documentaries, and films, each exploring different aspects of the heist and the ongoing search for the missing art. These works have contributed to the painting's legendary status, making it one of the most famous stolen artworks in history.

Conclusion: The Unsolved Enigma

The Case of the Vanished Vermeer stands as one of the greatest unsolved mysteries in the art world. Despite decades of investigation, the painting remains missing, and its fate is unknown. The story of this heist continues to captivate the imagination, not only because of the value of the stolen art but also because it touches on deeper themes of loss, memory, and the enduring power of art.

As long as "The Concert" remains missing, the case will continue to be a topic of fascination and speculation. The empty frame at the Isabella Stewart Gardner Museum serves as a silent witness to the crime, a reminder of what was taken and the ongoing quest to bring it back. The Vanished Vermeer is more than just a missing painting; it is a symbol of the enduring mystery and the unending search for answers in the world of art.

Chapter 21: The Mystery of the Missing Monet

The theft of a Claude Monet painting is not just the loss of a beautiful work of art; it is the disappearance of a piece of history, culture, and creativity. The case often referred to as "The Mystery of the Missing Monet" encapsulates the drama, intrigue, and frustration that surrounds art theft, particularly when it involves one of the most beloved artists in history. Claude Monet, the father of Impressionism, created works that are celebrated for their vibrant colors, delicate brushwork, and the ability to capture the ephemeral beauty of nature. The loss of one of his paintings represents not only a financial blow but also a profound cultural loss.

Claude Monet: The Master of Light and Landscape

Claude Monet, born in 1840, was a pioneering French painter who became the leading figure of the Impressionist movement. His works are known for their ability to capture light, color, and atmosphere, often depicting scenes of gardens, water lilies, and the changing effects of light on the landscape. Monet's paintings are characterized by their loose brushwork, which gives his works a sense of spontaneity and fluidity. His ability to capture the fleeting effects of light and weather has made his paintings some of the most beloved and valuable in the world.

Monet's influence on the art world cannot be overstated. His approach to painting, which focused on capturing the impression of a scene rather than its precise details, revolutionized the way artists approached their work. His series of paintings, such as the "Water Lilies," "Haystacks," and "Rouen Cathedral," are iconic, and his work continues to inspire artists and captivate audiences around the globe.

The Heist: A Bold Theft in Broad Daylight

The case of the missing Monet involves the daring theft of one of the artist's masterpieces. On October 22, 2012, thieves broke into the Kunsthal Museum in Rotterdam, Netherlands, and stole seven paintings, including Monet's "Waterloo Bridge, London" and "Charing Cross Bridge, London." These paintings were part of the Triton Foundation collection, a private collection that was on public display at the museum.

The thieves struck in the early hours of the morning, using what appeared to be a well-planned operation. They bypassed the museum's security system, which was criticized for its lack of robustness, and made off with the paintings in a matter of minutes. The stolen Monet paintings were particularly valuable, not only because of their artistic merit but also because they were part of a series that Monet painted during his stays in London. The "Waterloo Bridge" and "Charing Cross Bridge" paintings are renowned for their depiction of London's foggy atmosphere, with Monet's signature style bringing the scenes to life.

The Investigation: A Puzzle with Missing Pieces

The investigation into the Kunsthal Museum heist was immediate and intense. Dutch authorities, along with Interpol and other international agencies, launched a manhunt for the perpetrators. The theft was one of the most significant art heists in recent history, with the value of the stolen paintings estimated to be over $100 million. Despite the rapid response, the investigation faced numerous challenges.

The thieves had left behind few clues, and there was little physical evidence to work with. Security camera footage showed the masked intruders, but their identities remained unknown. Investigators explored various leads, including the possibility that the theft was orchestrated by organized crime groups, but progress was slow. The stolen paintings, including the Monet masterpieces, seemed to vanish without a trace.

The Global Hunt: Tracing the Monet Masterpieces

The search for the missing Monet paintings extended far beyond the borders of the Netherlands. Art theft is a global issue, and stolen masterpieces often find their way into the hands of private collectors, black markets, or are used as collateral in illegal dealings. As such, the investigation into the Kunsthal heist involved coordination with law enforcement agencies around the world.

Interpol issued international alerts for the stolen paintings, and the art world was on high alert. The theft of such high-profile works had a significant impact on the global art market, raising concerns about the security of cultural institutions and the vulnerability of even the most well-guarded collections. Despite the widespread efforts to recover the stolen art, months passed with no significant breakthroughs.

The Breakthrough: A Glimmer of Hope

In a surprising turn of events, Romanian authorities made a breakthrough in the case in 2013. Several suspects were arrested in connection with the Kunsthal heist, and it was revealed that the stolen paintings had been transported to Romania. The suspects were part of a criminal gang with a history of theft and smuggling. The arrests provided a glimmer of hope that the missing Monet paintings, along with the other stolen works, might be recovered.

However, the investigation took a tragic turn when one of the suspects' mothers claimed that she had burned the stolen paintings in an attempt to destroy evidence. The news sent shockwaves through the art world, as the loss of these masterpieces would be irreparable. Art experts and investigators were skeptical of the claim, as burning such valuable works would seem irrational, even for desperate criminals.

Nevertheless, the possibility that the Monet paintings had been destroyed added a layer of despair to the case.

The Uncertainty: Are the Monet Paintings Lost Forever?

Despite the arrests and the subsequent trial of the suspects, the fate of the missing Monet paintings remains uncertain. The claims of their destruction have never been fully verified, and no trace of the paintings has been found. The art world continues to hold out hope that the works are still out there, hidden away in some unknown location, waiting to be rediscovered.

The loss of these Monet paintings is not just a financial blow; it is a cultural tragedy. Monet's work is irreplaceable, and each painting represents a unique expression of his artistic vision. The thought that these masterpieces might have been destroyed is almost too painful to contemplate, and it underscores the devastating impact of art theft on our shared cultural heritage.

The Cultural Impact: A Loss Beyond Measure

The disappearance of Monet's "Waterloo Bridge, London" and "Charing Cross Bridge, London" has had a profound impact on the art world and beyond. These paintings are part of a larger series that Monet created during his visits to London, and their loss has left a significant gap in our understanding of his work during this period. Monet's London series is celebrated for its exploration of light, atmosphere, and the urban landscape, and each painting is a vital piece of this artistic puzzle.

The loss of these works is felt not only by art historians and collectors but also by the general public. Monet's paintings have a universal appeal, and their beauty transcends cultural and national boundaries. The theft and possible destruction of these masterpieces is a reminder of the fragility of our cultural heritage and the need to protect and preserve it for future generations.

The Art World's Response: Heightened Security and Vigilance

The Kunsthal heist, and the mystery of the missing Monet paintings, has had a lasting impact on the art world. Museums and galleries around the globe have taken steps to enhance security measures and protect their collections from similar thefts. The incident has also sparked discussions about the responsibilities of cultural institutions in safeguarding their treasures and the need for international cooperation in combating art theft.

In addition to physical security, the art world has also embraced technological advancements to track and recover stolen art. Digital databases, blockchain technology, and enhanced collaboration between law enforcement agencies and art experts have all contributed to a more robust approach to art crime. However, despite these efforts, the mystery of the missing Monet remains unsolved, a testament to the enduring challenge of recovering stolen art.

The Legacy of the Missing Monet: An Unsolved Enigma

The Mystery of the Missing Monet is more than just a case of stolen art; it is a story that touches on themes of loss, hope, and the enduring power of beauty. Monet's paintings, with their vibrant colors and masterful depiction of light, are a celebration of life and nature. Their loss is a blow to our collective cultural heritage, and the unresolved nature of the case adds to its poignancy.

As the years pass, the fate of the missing Monet paintings remains a haunting question. Were they truly destroyed, as claimed by the suspect's mother, or are they hidden away, waiting to be discovered? The possibility that these masterpieces might one day be recovered keeps the art world on edge, and the case continues to be a subject of fascination and speculation.

Conclusion: The Unfinished Story

The Mystery of the Missing Monet is an unfinished story, one that continues to intrigue and frustrate those who seek to uncover the truth. The loss of Monet's "Waterloo Bridge, London" and "Charing Cross Bridge, London" is a tragedy that extends beyond the art world, touching anyone who has ever been moved by the beauty of art.

The empty frames where these paintings once hung serve as a reminder of what was taken, and the ongoing search for answers reflects the human desire to recover what has been lost. As long as the mystery remains unsolved, the case of the missing Monet will continue to capture the imagination, a symbol of the enduring allure and elusiveness of art.

Chapter 22: The Puzzle of the Stolen Picasso

The theft of a Picasso painting is not merely the disappearance of a valuable piece of art; it is the vanishing of a fragment of modern art history. Pablo Picasso, a towering figure in 20th-century art, is often hailed as a genius who transformed artistic expression. His works, ranging from the bold and colorful to the abstract and provocative, are among the most sought-after in the world. The "Puzzle of the Stolen Picasso" delves into the intricate and perplexing world of art theft, focusing on one of the most notorious cases involving a Picasso masterpiece. This case epitomizes the challenges of protecting cultural treasures and the complexities of the global art market.

Pablo Picasso: A Revolutionary Artist

Pablo Picasso, born in 1881 in Málaga, Spain, was a prolific and innovative artist whose influence on modern art is immeasurable. Throughout his career, Picasso explored a wide range of styles and techniques, from the groundbreaking Cubism that he co-founded with Georges Braque to his later works that incorporated surrealism and abstraction. His paintings, sculptures, and prints are celebrated for their creativity, emotional depth, and bold departure from traditional artistic conventions.

Picasso's art is known for its ability to capture the complexities of the human experience, often reflecting the tumultuous events of the 20th century, including war, political upheaval, and personal struggle. His work spans over seven decades, and his contributions to art are vast and varied. With over 20,000 pieces attributed to him, Picasso's legacy is unparalleled, making his work highly coveted by collectors, museums, and unfortunately, thieves.

The Heist: A Daring Act of Deception

The Puzzle of the Stolen Picasso revolves around the theft of one of Picasso's iconic paintings. Among the many high-profile thefts of his work, one of the most audacious occurred in Paris on May 20, 2010. In the early hours of the morning, a lone thief broke into the Musée d'Art Moderne de la Ville de Paris and stole five paintings, including Picasso's "Le Pigeon aux Petits Pois" (The Pigeon with Green Peas). The thief, later dubbed "The Spider-Man," due to his ability to scale the museum's walls, entered through a window he had previously cut open and carefully removed the paintings from their frames.

The theft was discovered later that morning when museum staff found empty frames hanging on the walls. The stolen works, which included pieces by Henri Matisse, Georges Braque, Amedeo Modigliani, and Fernand Léger, were valued at around €100 million. Picasso's "Le Pigeon aux Petits Pois," a vibrant Cubist work painted in 1911, was one of the most valuable of the stolen paintings, estimated at €28 million.

The simplicity and precision of the heist were shocking. The thief bypassed the museum's alarm system, which had been malfunctioning for several weeks, and left no trace of his identity. The theft was a major embarrassment for the museum and raised serious questions about the security of cultural institutions in Paris. The heist also set off a global manhunt, as law enforcement agencies scrambled to recover the stolen masterpieces.

The Investigation: Unraveling a Complex Web

The investigation into the theft was swift and intense, with French police, Interpol, and art crime specialists working together to track down the stolen Picasso and other artworks. Initial suspicions centered on the possibility that the theft was orchestrated by a sophisticated criminal network, given the high value and the specific targeting of the paintings. Investigators explored various leads, including the potential involvement of organized crime and the black market for stolen art.

Despite the extensive efforts, the investigation faced significant challenges. The thief had left few clues, and the paintings seemed to have vanished without a trace. In the days and weeks following the theft, numerous rumors circulated about the whereabouts of the stolen art. Some speculated that the paintings had been smuggled out of France and were being held in a private collection, while others believed that the thief might have been acting on behalf of a wealthy art collector.

The case took a dramatic turn in 2011 when a suspect was arrested in connection with the theft. Vjeran Tomic, a 49-year-old Serbian national, was apprehended after a tip-off led police to his apartment in Paris. Known in criminal circles as "Spider-Man" for his acrobatic abilities, Tomic had a history of art theft and was suspected of being behind the Musée d'Art Moderne heist. During his interrogation, Tomic admitted to the theft, claiming that he had acted alone and had initially targeted the museum for a different painting but decided to steal multiple works when he saw the opportunity.

Tomic's arrest was a breakthrough in the case, but it did not immediately lead to the recovery of the stolen paintings. During the investigation, Tomic revealed that he had passed the stolen Picasso and other artworks to an accomplice, who had then sold them to an unknown buyer. Despite extensive searches and further arrests, the whereabouts of the paintings remained unknown. The confession added to the complexity of the puzzle, as investigators now had to unravel the network of individuals involved in the sale and distribution of the stolen art.

The Search for "Le Pigeon aux Petits Pois": A Global Effort

The hunt for Picasso's "Le Pigeon aux Petits Pois" became a global pursuit, involving art experts, detectives, and even private investigators. The theft highlighted the difficulties of recovering stolen art, particularly when it comes to works by artists as famous as Picasso. Stolen masterpieces often disappear into the shadowy world of black-market art dealing, where they can be used as collateral in illegal transactions, traded between criminals, or hidden away by wealthy collectors.

Interpol and other international agencies issued alerts for the stolen paintings, and the case received widespread media coverage. The theft of such high-profile works drew attention not only to the weaknesses in museum security but also to the broader issue of art theft, which has been described as one of the largest black markets in the world, second only to drug trafficking.

The investigation was further complicated by the nature of Picasso's work. Due to the sheer volume of Picasso's output and the various styles he explored throughout his career, it can be challenging to authenticate and trace his paintings, especially when they are sold on the black market. "Le Pigeon aux Petits Pois" is a distinctive Cubist work, but in the chaotic world of illegal art dealing, even such a recognizable piece can vanish.

The Mystery Deepens: False Leads and Dead Ends

As the search for the stolen Picasso continued, investigators encountered numerous false leads and dead ends. Various individuals came forward claiming to have information about the painting's whereabouts, but these tips often led to nowhere. In some cases, the information provided was part of elaborate scams, with individuals attempting to extort money in exchange for false details about the missing art.

In 2013, a breakthrough seemed imminent when French police received information that the stolen paintings had been smuggled out of France and were being held in a warehouse in Serbia. However, when authorities raided the location, they found no trace of the missing Picasso or the other artworks. This false lead was a significant setback in the investigation and highlighted the challenges of navigating the complex world of international art crime.

The frustration of the investigators was palpable, as each new lead seemed to bring them closer to solving the puzzle, only for it to unravel again. The continued absence of the paintings cast a long shadow over the case, and doubts began to grow about whether the stolen art would ever be recovered.

The Cultural Impact: A Loss Felt Worldwide

The theft of Picasso's "Le Pigeon aux Petits Pois" and the other paintings was not just a financial loss; it was a cultural tragedy. Picasso's work is a cornerstone of modern art, and the loss of even a single painting represents a significant blow to the art world. Museums, galleries, and the general public were deprived of the opportunity to experience these masterpieces, and the theft raised important questions about the security and preservation of cultural heritage.

The disappearance of these works also had a profound impact on the art market. The theft underscored the vulnerabilities of even the most prestigious institutions and led to increased scrutiny of museum security practices worldwide. In response, many museums implemented stricter security measures, including the use of advanced surveillance technology, increased physical security, and better coordination with law enforcement agencies.

The case also sparked a broader discussion about the value of art and the motivations behind art theft. While some thieves are motivated by the potential financial gain, others are driven by a desire to possess and control something of immense cultural and emotional value. The theft of a Picasso is not just a crime; it is an act that touches on deeper themes of ownership, legacy, and the human desire to leave a mark on history.

The Legacy of the Stolen Picasso: A Lingering Mystery

The Puzzle of the Stolen Picasso remains unsolved, a haunting reminder of the complexities of art theft and the challenges of recovering stolen masterpieces. Despite the arrest of Vjeran Tomic and the efforts of law enforcement agencies around the world, Picasso's "Le Pigeon aux Petits Pois" has never been recovered. The painting's fate is unknown, and its absence leaves a gap in the history of modern art.

The continued mystery surrounding the stolen Picasso has kept the case in the public eye. It serves as a symbol of the enduring allure and elusiveness of art, as well as the lengths to which individuals will go to possess something of such immense value. The empty frame where "Le Pigeon aux Petits Pois" once hung is a poignant reminder of what was lost, and the ongoing search for the painting reflects the human desire to restore what has been taken.

In the years since the theft, the case has inspired books, documentaries, and countless discussions in the art world. The story of the stolen Picasso is not just a tale of crime; it is a narrative that speaks to the broader themes of loss, recovery, and the enduring power of art. The painting itself, with its vibrant colors and intricate Cubist forms, is a testament to Picasso's genius, and its disappearance is a loss that resonates far beyond the walls of the Musée d'Art Moderne.

Conclusion: The Unfinished Puzzle

The Puzzle of the Stolen Picasso remains an unfinished puzzle, a story with missing pieces and unanswered questions. The theft of "Le Pigeon aux Petits Pois" is a case that continues to captivate and confound those who seek to understand it. The painting's fate is a mystery, and the search for it is a quest that continues to this day.

As time passes, the hope of recovering the stolen Picasso diminishes, but the case remains a powerful reminder of the fragility of cultural heritage and the challenges of protecting it. The story of the stolen Picasso is not just about a missing painting; it is about the enduring impact of art and the lengths to which people will go to possess and control it. As long as the painting remains missing, the puzzle will remain unsolved, a lingering mystery that continues to haunt the world of art.

Chapter 23: The Hunt for the Missing Fabergé Eggs

The mystery of the missing Fabergé eggs is one of the most captivating tales in the world of art and antiquities. These exquisite creations, crafted by the House of Fabergé in the late 19th and early 20th centuries, are among the most coveted treasures of the Russian imperial family. Originally commissioned by the Russian Tsars as opulent Easter gifts for their families, the Fabergé eggs represent the pinnacle of luxury, artistry, and craftsmanship. However, in the chaos following the Russian Revolution and the collapse of the Romanov dynasty, several of these priceless eggs vanished, sparking a century-long hunt that has fascinated collectors, historians, and treasure hunters alike.

The Origin of the Fabergé Eggs: A Symbol of Imperial Grandeur

The story of the Fabergé eggs begins in 1885, when Tsar Alexander III of Russia commissioned the first of these extraordinary creations as a gift for his wife, Empress Maria Feodorovna, to celebrate Easter. The egg, known as the "Hen Egg," was a masterpiece of intricate design and craftsmanship. On the outside, it appeared to be a simple enameled egg, but inside, it held a series of surprises: a golden yolk, within which was a golden hen, which in turn contained a miniature replica of the imperial crown and a tiny ruby pendant.

The Empress was so delighted with the gift that the Tsar decided to commission a Fabergé egg every year thereafter, a tradition that was continued by his son, Tsar Nicholas II. Each year, Fabergé and his team of master craftsmen created a new egg, each more elaborate and intricate than the last, featuring a unique design and often containing a hidden surprise. These eggs became symbols of the wealth, power, and opulence of the Romanov dynasty, and they were cherished by the imperial family.

Over the course of three decades, from 1885 to 1917, the House of Fabergé created a total of 50 imperial eggs, each one a masterpiece of artistry and engineering. These eggs were not merely decorative objects; they were complex, jewel-encrusted creations that showcased the extraordinary skill of Fabergé's craftsmen. The eggs incorporated a wide range of precious materials, including gold, silver, platinum, diamonds, and rare gemstones, as well as innovative techniques such as enamel work, guilloché (a decorative technique involving intricate, repetitive patterns), and mechanical engineering to create moving parts.

The Russian Revolution and the Disappearance of the Eggs

The opulent world of the Russian imperial family came to an abrupt and tragic end with the Russian Revolution of 1917. The Bolsheviks, led by Vladimir Lenin, overthrew the Romanov dynasty, and Tsar Nicholas II, along with his family, was imprisoned and eventually executed. The treasures of the imperial family, including the Fabergé eggs, were seized by the new Soviet government.

In the aftermath of the revolution, the fate of the Fabergé eggs became increasingly uncertain. The Bolsheviks, eager to raise funds for their fledgling regime, began selling off the imperial treasures to foreign buyers. Many of the Fabergé eggs were sold to wealthy collectors in Europe and the United States, while others were kept in Soviet museums. However, amid the chaos and secrecy of the time, some of the eggs disappeared, their whereabouts unknown.

Of the 50 imperial Fabergé eggs created, 43 are known to have survived, with some held in museums and others in private collections. However, seven of these imperial eggs remain missing, their fate shrouded in mystery. These missing eggs include the "Hen with Sapphire Pendant" (1886), the "Cherub with Chariot" (1888), the "Necessaire" (1889), the "Egg with Alexander III Portraits" (1896), the "Renaissance" (1894), the "Mauve" (1897), and the "Royal Danish" (1903). Additionally, several non-imperial Fabergé eggs, created for private clients, have also vanished over the years.

The Hunt Begins: Collectors and Connoisseurs on the Trail

The hunt for the missing Fabergé eggs has been a pursuit filled with intrigue, speculation, and occasional breakthroughs. Collectors, historians, and treasure hunters have scoured archives, auction records, and private collections in search of clues that might lead to the discovery of these lost masterpieces.

One of the most famous breakthroughs in the search for the missing eggs occurred in 2014, when a scrap-metal dealer in the United States made an astonishing discovery. The dealer had purchased a gold egg at a flea market for $14,000, hoping to sell it for scrap value. However, after noticing a Vacheron Constantin watch inside the egg, he decided to research the piece further. To his amazement, he discovered that the egg was one of the missing Fabergé imperial eggs, specifically the "Third Imperial Egg," which had been lost for over a century. The egg, created in 1887, was later sold to a private collector for an undisclosed sum, reportedly around $33 million.

This remarkable discovery reignited interest in the search for the remaining missing eggs. The story of the "Third Imperial Egg" underscored the fact that these treasures could be hidden in plain sight, perhaps languishing in forgotten collections or overlooked by those who do not realize their true value.

Theories and Speculation: Where Are the Missing Eggs?

Theories about the whereabouts of the missing Fabergé eggs abound, ranging from the plausible to the fantastical. Some experts believe that the missing eggs may still be hidden in Russia, possibly in private collections or in state repositories that have not been fully cataloged.

The chaotic period following the Russian Revolution saw many treasures lost, hidden, or misappropriated, and it is possible that some of the missing eggs remain in the country, awaiting rediscovery.

Others speculate that the missing eggs were smuggled out of Russia during the revolution or the subsequent civil war and sold to private collectors in Europe or the United States. Given the secrecy and discretion that often surrounds high-end art transactions, it is conceivable that the missing eggs have changed hands multiple times over the years, with each new owner unaware of the object's true provenance.

There is also the possibility that some of the missing eggs have been lost to history, destroyed during the turmoil of the revolution or the ravages of war. The "Hen with Sapphire Pendant," for example, was last recorded in the possession of the Soviet government in 1922, but no trace of it has been found since. Similarly, the "Mauve" egg, gifted to Empress Alexandra Feodorovna in 1897, has not been seen since it was sent to the Kremlin Armoury for safekeeping in 1917.

Despite these uncertainties, the search for the missing Fabergé eggs continues, driven by the allure of these extraordinary objects and the hope that they may yet be found.

The Cultural and Artistic Significance of the Fabergé Eggs

The Fabergé eggs are more than just luxurious objects; they are cultural artifacts that encapsulate the history, artistry, and craftsmanship of a bygone era. Each egg is a testament to the skill and creativity of the artisans who crafted them, as well as a reflection of the tastes and aspirations of the Russian imperial family.

The eggs are also significant for their role in the broader history of decorative arts and jewelry. Fabergé's work represents a fusion of different artistic traditions, including Russian, French, and Renaissance influences, and the eggs themselves are masterpieces of design and engineering. The use of precious materials, intricate enameling, and mechanical surprises within the eggs set new standards for luxury objects and continue to inspire admiration and awe.

The loss of any Fabergé egg is a significant cultural tragedy, as each one represents a unique intersection of art, history, and craftsmanship. The missing eggs, in particular, have taken on an almost mythical status in the world of art and antiquities, their absence only adding to their allure.

The Modern-Day Search: Technology and New Approaches

In recent years, advancements in technology and new approaches to art recovery have renewed hopes that the missing Fabergé eggs might still be found. Databases of stolen and missing art, such as the Art Loss Register, have become invaluable tools for tracking and recovering lost treasures. Additionally, advances in digital imaging and analysis have allowed researchers to study existing photographs and records of the missing eggs in greater detail, potentially uncovering new leads.

Private collectors and museums have also played a crucial role in the search. Some collectors have made their Fabergé collections publicly accessible, allowing experts to study the pieces and compare them with historical records. Museums and galleries have also been instrumental in raising awareness about the missing eggs, hosting exhibitions and lectures that highlight their significance and the ongoing search.

Another important aspect of the modern-day search is the increased cooperation between governments, law enforcement agencies, and private organizations. International efforts to combat art theft and recover lost cultural property have intensified in recent years, with greater collaboration across borders. This has led to the recovery of numerous lost or stolen artworks, and it is hoped that similar efforts will eventually lead to the discovery of the missing Fabergé eggs.

The Legacy of the Missing Fabergé Eggs

The legacy of the missing Fabergé eggs extends beyond the realm of art and antiquities. These lost treasures are emblematic of the broader challenges of preserving cultural heritage in times of political and social upheaval. The eggs serve as poignant reminders of the fragility of human achievements and the importance of safeguarding our shared cultural history.

The story of the missing eggs also underscores the enduring fascination with the Romanov dynasty and the opulence of the Russian imperial court. The eggs are inextricably linked to the history of the Romanovs, and their disappearance is a symbol of the tragic fate that befell the family and their empire.

For those involved in the hunt, the search for the missing Fabergé eggs is more than just a quest for valuable objects; it is a mission to restore lost history and reconnect with the past. Each discovery, no matter how small, brings us closer to understanding the full story of these extraordinary creations and the world that produced them.

Conclusion: The Unfinished Journey

The hunt for the missing Fabergé eggs is an unfinished journey, a quest that continues to captivate and intrigue. As long as these treasures remain lost, the search will go on, driven by the hope that they may one day be found and returned to their rightful place in the annals of history.

The missing Fabergé eggs are more than just objects of beauty and value; they are symbols of a lost world, relics of an era that has passed into history. Their recovery would not only be a triumph for art and culture but also a poignant reminder of the impermanence of even the most exquisite creations.

The story of the missing Fabergé eggs is a tale of loss and discovery, of mystery and intrigue. It is a story that continues to unfold, with each new lead and each new discovery adding another chapter to the saga. And as long as the eggs remain missing, the hunt will continue, driven by the enduring allure of these imperial treasures.

Chapter 24: The World's Greatest Wine Theft

The world of fine wine is one of luxury, sophistication, and, at times, intrigue. Among the countless stories that populate the annals of viniculture, the saga of the world's greatest wine theft stands out as a particularly audacious and meticulously executed crime. This heist, involving the theft of some of the most expensive and rare wines ever produced, has left a lasting mark on both the wine industry and the world of high-stakes thefts. The theft not only exposed vulnerabilities in the security of even the most exclusive establishments but also highlighted the lengths to which some individuals will go to obtain a taste of the world's most coveted vintages.

The Scene of the Crime: A Prestigious Venue and Its Prized Collection

The setting for the world's greatest wine theft was not a dusty wine cellar or a forgotten storage facility but rather one of the most prestigious wine collections in the world. This theft took place at the famed Hôtel de Crillon in Paris, a luxurious establishment that housed one of the most impressive collections of fine wines and spirits. The hotel, renowned for its opulence and history, was home to a wine cellar that contained some of the rarest and most valuable bottles in existence.

The cellar at the Hôtel de Crillon was a treasure trove for wine connoisseurs, with its collection spanning centuries and including bottles from legendary vineyards such as Château Lafite Rothschild, Château Margaux, and Domaine de la Romanée-Conti. These wines, some of which dated back to the early 19th century, were not only valuable due to their rarity but also because of their historical significance. Each bottle represented a piece of vinicultural history, a testament to the artistry and dedication of winemakers across generations.

The Heist: A Masterclass in Precision and Planning

The theft was a meticulously planned operation, executed with precision and care. Unlike many high-profile heists that rely on brute force or hurried actions, this crime was the work of individuals who understood the value of the items they were targeting and took the time to ensure their success. The thieves were not only skilled but also patient, waiting for the perfect moment to strike.

On the night of the theft, the perpetrators gained access to the wine cellar through a series of carefully orchestrated steps. They bypassed security systems, avoided detection by surveillance cameras, and used specialized tools to open the locked doors of the cellar. Once inside, they were selective in their choices, targeting only the most valuable bottles. This selective approach indicated that the thieves were knowledgeable about fine wines and knew exactly what they were looking for.

Over the course of several hours, the thieves removed numerous bottles of rare and valuable wine, carefully packing them into crates to avoid damaging the fragile contents. By the time they left the Hôtel de Crillon, they had stolen millions of dollars' worth of wine, including some of the rarest vintages in the world.

The Aftermath: A Shockwave Through the Wine World

The discovery of the theft sent shockwaves through the wine industry and the world of luxury goods. The Hôtel de Crillon, known for its impeccable reputation and stringent security measures, was now the scene of one of the most audacious thefts in history. The stolen wine, estimated to be worth between $3 million and $5 million, represented not just a financial loss but a cultural one as well. Some of the bottles taken were irreplaceable, with no remaining examples left in existence.

The investigation into the theft was swift and involved multiple law enforcement agencies, including the French police and Interpol. The authorities were keenly aware of the challenges they faced in recovering the stolen wine. Unlike stolen jewelry or art, which can be relatively easy to track due to their unique characteristics, stolen wine presents a different set of challenges. Bottles can be consumed, labels can be altered, and provenance can be difficult to verify, especially if the thieves were to sell the wine on the black market.

The heist also raised concerns about the security of other high-value wine collections around the world. Collectors, restaurateurs, and wine merchants were suddenly forced to reevaluate their security measures, recognizing that even the most prestigious establishments were not immune to such crimes. The theft at the Hôtel de Crillon served as a wake-up call, prompting many to invest in more sophisticated security systems, including biometric locks, advanced surveillance technology, and even armed guards.

The Investigation: Unraveling the Web of Deception

As the investigation into the wine theft unfolded, it became clear that this was not the work of amateur criminals. The level of sophistication and planning involved suggested that the perpetrators were experienced and well-connected within the world of high-value thefts. The police began to piece together clues, examining the methods used to bypass the hotel's security and interviewing staff members who might have unwittingly provided information to the thieves.

One of the key challenges in the investigation was tracing the stolen wine. Given the value of the bottles, it was unlikely that the thieves would attempt to sell them on the open market, where they would quickly attract attention. Instead, the authorities suspected that the wine might be sold through private channels, either to unscrupulous collectors or through underground networks specializing in luxury goods.

To complicate matters further, the police had to consider the possibility that the wine had been stolen to order, with the thieves acting on behalf of a wealthy client who wanted to add these rare bottles to their private collection. In such a scenario, the chances of recovering the stolen wine would be slim, as the bottles would likely remain hidden in a private cellar, out of reach of the authorities.

Despite these challenges, the investigation continued, with the police following leads across Europe and beyond. They conducted raids on known black-market dealers, monitored auctions and private sales of fine wine, and even enlisted the help of wine experts to identify any bottles that might have been part of the stolen haul. The case also drew the attention of private investigators, hired by the hotel's insurers to assist in the search for the missing wine.

The Impact on the Wine Industry: A New Era of Vigilance

The impact of the world's greatest wine theft was felt far beyond the walls of the Hôtel de Crillon. In the wake of the heist, the wine industry underwent a significant transformation, with a renewed focus on security and provenance. Collectors and merchants alike recognized the need to protect their investments, leading to a surge in demand for secure storage facilities and insurance coverage for fine wines.

The theft also highlighted the growing issue of wine fraud, a problem that has plagued the industry for decades. As the value of fine wine has increased, so too has the prevalence of counterfeit bottles and fraudulent transactions. The theft at the Hôtel de Crillon underscored the importance of verifying the authenticity of wine and ensuring that proper documentation and provenance records are maintained.

In response to these concerns, new technologies have been developed to combat wine fraud and improve security. For example, some wineries and collectors have begun using blockchain technology to create tamper-proof records of a wine's history, from the vineyard to the bottle. This digital ledger provides an immutable record of the wine's provenance, making it more difficult for counterfeiters to pass off fake bottles as the real thing.

In addition, some collectors have turned to high-tech solutions such as RFID tags and smart bottle caps, which can track the location and condition of a bottle in real-time. These innovations provide an added layer of security, allowing collectors to monitor their investments and detect any unauthorized access to their wine collections.

The Cultural Significance: Wine as an Object of Desire

The world's greatest wine theft is more than just a story of crime and intrigue; it is a reflection of the cultural significance of wine and its role as an object of desire. Fine wine has long been associated with luxury, status, and sophistication, and the theft of such rare and valuable bottles speaks to the lengths to which people will go to obtain these symbols of wealth and prestige.

Wine, particularly rare vintages from renowned vineyards, is not just a beverage; it is a collector's item, a piece of history, and a work of art. The allure of owning a bottle of wine that has been aged for decades, or even centuries, is a powerful draw for collectors and connoisseurs. For some, the value of a bottle goes beyond its monetary worth; it is about the experience of tasting a piece of history, of savoring a wine that has been crafted with care and patience.

The theft of such wines is therefore not just a financial crime but a cultural one as well. The stolen bottles represent a loss of heritage, a disruption of the narrative that these wines tell. Each bottle is a story in itself, a reflection of the time, place, and people who produced it. When a bottle is stolen, that story is interrupted, and the connection between the past and the present is severed.

The Aftermath: Lessons Learned and the Ongoing Search

The aftermath of the world's greatest wine theft is a story of lessons learned and ongoing challenges. While the investigation into the theft at the Hôtel de Crillon eventually led to the recovery of some of the stolen bottles, many remain missing, their fate unknown. The heist served as a reminder of the vulnerabilities that exist even in the most secure environments and the need for constant vigilance in protecting valuable assets.

For the wine industry, the theft was a catalyst for change, prompting a reevaluation of security practices and the adoption of new technologies to safeguard valuable collections. It also sparked a renewed interest in the provenance of wine, with collectors becoming more aware of the importance of verifying the authenticity and history of the bottles they acquire.

The heist also left a lasting impact on the Hôtel de Crillon, which took extensive measures to improve its security in the wake of the theft. The hotel, once a symbol of luxury and refinement, now found itself at the center of a high-profile crime, its reputation temporarily tarnished by the incident. However, the hotel has since recovered, continuing to serve as a beacon of Parisian elegance and sophistication.

As for the stolen wine, the search continues. While some bottles have been recovered, others remain missing, their whereabouts a mystery. The stolen wine has likely changed hands many times, moving through underground networks and private sales, its true value recognized only by those who understand its significance.

The world's greatest wine theft is a story that continues to captivate, a tale of crime, culture, and the enduring allure of fine wine. It is a reminder that even in a world of luxury and refinement, the desire for rare and valuable objects can lead to acts of audacious criminality. And as long as there are those who covet the world's finest vintages, the risk of theft will remain, a shadow that lingers over the world of fine wine.

Chapter 25: The Brink's Armored Car Coup

The Brink's Armored Car Coup, often referred to as the "crime of the century," was a meticulously planned and daring robbery that took place on January 17, 1950, in Boston, Massachusetts. This heist not only captured the imagination of the American public but also set a new benchmark for criminal ingenuity. The audacity and precision of the robbery left law enforcement agencies scrambling for clues, and the ensuing investigation became one of the most extensive manhunts in U.S. history. The Brink's robbery remains one of the most famous and significant heists of all time, both for the amount of money stolen and the elaborate planning that went into executing the crime.

Setting the Stage: Post-War America and the Rise of Organized Crime

In the years following World War II, America was undergoing a period of rapid economic growth and prosperity. However, this era of affluence also saw a rise in organized crime, as criminal syndicates and gangs sought to capitalize on the booming economy. Cities like Boston were no exception, with various criminal elements vying for control of lucrative rackets, including gambling, loan-sharking, and theft.

The Brink's Armored Car Depot, located in the North End of Boston, was a key hub for the transportation and storage of large sums of money. Brink's, a company known for its security services, was responsible for transporting cash and valuables for banks, businesses, and government institutions. The armored car depot was considered one of the most secure facilities in the city, equipped with state-of-the-art alarms, heavy steel doors, and armed guards. However, the very fact that it was so secure made it an attractive target for a group of criminals who were determined to pull off the perfect heist.

The Masterminds: A Crew of Seasoned Criminals

The Brink's robbery was not the work of a single mastermind but rather a team of seasoned criminals who brought their own unique skills and expertise to the table. The group consisted of eleven men, all of whom had extensive criminal backgrounds, including robbery, burglary, and other forms of organized crime. The leader of the gang was Tony "Fats" Pino, a notorious career criminal with a reputation for planning and executing high-stakes heists. Pino was known for his meticulous attention to detail and his ability to assemble a team of skilled criminals.

Among the other key members of the gang were Joseph "Specs" O'Keefe, a safecracker with a talent for bypassing complex security systems; Stanley "Gus" Gusciora, an experienced getaway driver; and Vincent "Fat Vinnie" Costa, a burglar with a knack for evading capture. Each member of the crew was carefully chosen for their specific skills, and together, they formed a formidable team capable of taking on the most challenging of heists.

The planning for the Brink's robbery began nearly two years before the actual crime took place. During this time, the gang conducted extensive surveillance of the Brink's depot, studying the movements of the guards, the layout of the building, and the security measures in place. They also gathered detailed information on the schedules of the armored car deliveries and the amounts of money stored in the vaults. This meticulous planning would prove to be a crucial factor in the success of the heist.

The Heist: Precision, Timing, and Execution

On the evening of January 17, 1950, the gang put their plan into action. Disguised in navy peacoats, chauffeur caps, and Halloween masks to conceal their identities, the criminals approached the Brink's depot. They had chosen this specific time because they knew that the guards would be in the process of closing up for the night, which meant that the vault would be open and access to the money would be easier.

The gang entered the building through a side door that they had previously unlocked during one of their earlier reconnaissance missions. Once inside, they quickly overpowered the guards, tying them up and blindfolding them to prevent them from identifying the robbers. The gang members worked with military-like precision, moving swiftly to the vault where the money was stored.

Using their insider knowledge of the depot's layout and security measures, the gang managed to open the vault without triggering any alarms. They then began loading the money into bags, working quickly but carefully to avoid leaving any evidence behind. In total, they stole $2.7 million in cash, checks, and money orders, a staggering sum at the time, equivalent to approximately $30 million today.

The entire heist took less than half an hour, and by the time the gang left the building, they had pulled off one of the most successful and lucrative robberies in history. The precision and efficiency with which the crime was carried out left law enforcement agencies baffled, as the robbers had managed to avoid leaving any fingerprints, footprints, or other traceable evidence.

The Aftermath: A National Sensation and a Relentless Investigation

The discovery of the robbery the next morning sent shockwaves through the city of Boston and quickly became a national sensation. The sheer audacity of the crime, combined with the enormous sum of money stolen, captured the public's imagination. Newspapers dubbed it the "crime of the century," and the FBI quickly took over the investigation.

Despite the lack of physical evidence, the FBI launched a massive manhunt for the perpetrators, interviewing thousands of suspects and conducting extensive surveillance on known criminals in the area. The investigation was one of the largest and most complex in the bureau's history, with agents working tirelessly to track down leads and gather information.

One of the key challenges facing the FBI was the fact that the gang members had carefully avoided spending any of the stolen money, knowing that doing so would attract attention and potentially lead to their capture. Instead, the gang members kept the money hidden, waiting for the heat from the investigation to die down before they attempted to use their ill-gotten gains.

However, as time passed, tensions within the gang began to rise. The pressure of keeping such a large secret, combined with the fear of being caught, led to infighting and paranoia among the group. In particular, Joseph "Specs" O'Keefe, who had been one of the key members of the heist, began to grow increasingly anxious and paranoid. He feared that the other gang members were planning to kill him to prevent him from talking to the authorities.

In 1954, four years after the robbery, O'Keefe was arrested on unrelated charges and, facing a long prison sentence, decided to cooperate with the FBI. He provided the authorities with detailed information about the heist and the identities of his accomplices, leading to the eventual arrest of the remaining gang members.

The Trial: Justice Served and the End of an Era

The trial of the Brink's gang was one of the most high-profile criminal cases of the 1950s. The evidence against the defendants, combined with O'Keefe's testimony, made it clear that the men on trial were responsible for the robbery. The trial attracted widespread media attention, with the public eager to learn more about the men who had pulled off the "crime of the century."

In October 1956, six years after the robbery, the members of the Brink's gang were convicted and sentenced to long prison terms. The trial marked the end of one of the most sensational crime stories in American history and brought a sense of closure to a case that had captivated the nation.

However, despite the convictions, only a small portion of the stolen money was ever recovered. The rest of the loot, estimated to be worth millions of dollars, was never found, leading to speculation that it had been hidden or laundered by the gang members before their capture. The mystery of what happened to the majority of the stolen money has continued to intrigue historians and true crime enthusiasts for decades.

The Legacy: The Brink's Heist in Popular Culture

The Brink's Armored Car Coup has left an indelible mark on American popular culture, serving as the inspiration for numerous books, movies, and television shows. The story of the heist, with its elements of meticulous planning, daring execution, and eventual downfall, has made it one of the most iconic crime stories in history.

One of the most famous portrayals of the Brink's robbery is the 1978 film *The Brink's Job*, directed by William Friedkin and starring Peter Falk as Tony Pino. The film, while taking some liberties with the facts, provides a dramatized account of the heist and the subsequent investigation. The Brink's robbery has also been the subject of numerous documentaries and true crime television series, which have explored the details of the crime and its impact on American law enforcement.

The heist has also influenced the depiction of criminal masterminds in popular culture, with the Brink's gang serving as a prototype for the cunning and resourceful criminals often portrayed in heist films and novels. The meticulous planning and precision of the robbery have made it a touchstone for those interested in the art of the heist, and the story continues to resonate with audiences today.

The Brink's Legacy: Lessons Learned and the Evolution of Security

The Brink's Armored Car Coup had a lasting impact on the security industry, leading to significant changes in the way armored car services and secure facilities operate. The heist exposed vulnerabilities in the security measures of the time, prompting companies like Brink's to adopt more advanced technologies and procedures to protect their assets.

In the years following the robbery, Brink's and other security firms invested heavily in improving their systems, including the introduction of more sophisticated alarm systems, reinforced vaults, and stricter access controls. The heist also underscored the importance of employee screening and internal security, as it became clear that insider knowledge had played a crucial role in the success of the crime.

Law enforcement agencies also learned valuable lessons from the Brink's case, particularly in the areas of investigation and surveillance. The FBI's extensive manhunt and use of informants in the Brink's case became a model for future investigations of organized crime and large-scale heists.

The Brink's robbery also highlighted the challenges of recovering stolen assets, especially in cases where the criminals are able to hide or launder the proceeds of their crimes. The case served as a reminder that even the most secure facilities are not immune to the ingenuity and determination of criminals, and that security measures must constantly evolve to keep pace with new threats.

Conclusion: The Brink's Heist as a Cautionary Tale

The Brink's Armored Car Coup remains one of the most famous and influential heists in history, a crime that not only captivated the public but also left a lasting legacy on the security industry and law enforcement. The story of the Brink's gang, with its blend of audacity, precision, and ultimate downfall, serves as a cautionary tale about the risks and rewards of criminal enterprise.

The heist is a reminder that even the most meticulously planned crimes are not without their flaws, and that the pursuit of wealth through illegal means often comes with a heavy price. For the members of the Brink's gang, the promise of easy money ultimately led to years of imprisonment and the loss of their freedom.

Today, the Brink's heist is remembered not only for the audacity of the crime but also for the lessons it taught about security, law enforcement, and the nature of criminal enterprise. It is a story that continues to resonate with audiences, a testament to the enduring allure of the heist genre and the fascination with those who dare to challenge the boundaries of the law.

Chapter 26: The Lost Bullion of the Spanish Main

The legend of the Lost Bullion of the Spanish Main is one of the most enduring and tantalizing stories of buried treasure in maritime history. It conjures images of galleons laden with gold, daring pirates, and secret islands where unimaginable wealth lies hidden beneath the sands. This tale, steeped in the history of the Spanish Empire's vast wealth and the turbulent waters of the Caribbean, continues to captivate treasure hunters, historians, and adventurers alike. It is a story that weaves together the threads of colonial ambition, piracy, and the relentless pursuit of lost riches.

The Spanish Main: The Golden Era of Empire and Wealth

The Spanish Main refers to the mainland coastal regions of the Spanish Empire in the Americas, primarily along the northern coast of South America, including present-day Venezuela, Colombia, and Panama. During the 16th and 17th centuries, this area became a central hub for Spanish colonial activities, particularly the extraction of vast quantities of gold, silver, and other precious commodities from the New World.

The wealth extracted from the Spanish Main played a crucial role in fueling the Spanish Empire's dominance in Europe. Gold and silver mined from the Americas were transported to the coast, where they were loaded onto treasure fleets bound for Spain. These fleets, known as the Spanish treasure galleons, sailed annually from the ports of the Spanish Main, heavily guarded against potential attacks by pirates and rival European powers.

The Spanish Empire's wealth became a target for these seafaring outlaws, who prowled the Caribbean Sea in search of plunder. The golden age of piracy, which spanned from the late 17th century to the early 18th century, saw an increase in attacks on Spanish ships and settlements. The legendary pirates of the Caribbean, such as Blackbeard, Henry Morgan, and Calico Jack, made their fortunes by looting Spanish galleons and coastal towns.

The Lost Bullion: Fact, Fiction, and the Birth of a Legend

The story of the Lost Bullion of the Spanish Main is rooted in the history of these treasure-laden ships, which were often vulnerable to storms, shipwrecks, and pirate attacks. One of the most famous incidents involving lost Spanish treasure occurred in 1715, when a fleet of eleven Spanish galleons was caught in a hurricane off the coast of Florida. The ships, which were heavily laden with gold, silver, and jewels, were bound for Spain after having collected a year's worth of treasure from the colonies.

The hurricane decimated the fleet, sinking the majority of the ships and scattering their valuable cargo along the Florida coastline and into the depths of the ocean. This event became known as the 1715 Treasure Fleet disaster, and it is one of the most significant shipwrecks in history, with much of the treasure still lying undiscovered beneath the sea.

The loss of the 1715 fleet is just one example of how the bullion and riches of the Spanish Main were lost to the depths. Over the centuries, numerous other galleons met similar fates, whether due to natural disasters or attacks by pirates. These lost treasures gave rise to countless legends and stories, with the promise of untold riches waiting to be found by those brave or lucky enough to discover them.

Pirates and Plunder: The Pursuit of Spanish Treasure

Pirates played a central role in the story of the Lost Bullion of the Spanish Main. These seafaring bandits thrived in the warm waters of the Caribbean, where the vast wealth of the Spanish Empire provided ample opportunity for plunder. The Caribbean became a pirate's paradise, with its maze of islands, hidden coves, and treacherous reefs offering ideal hiding places for both pirates and their stolen loot.

The pirates who hunted the Spanish treasure fleets were notorious for their ruthlessness and cunning. Figures like Captain William Kidd, who was initially commissioned as a privateer to protect British interests, turned to piracy and amassed vast fortunes by attacking Spanish ships. Another infamous pirate, Bartholomew Roberts, known as Black Bart, captured hundreds of ships during his career, many of them Spanish vessels carrying treasure from the New World.

These pirates not only attacked ships but also targeted Spanish coastal settlements, where they could raid the storehouses and strongholds where treasure was kept before being shipped to Europe. The sacking of Panama by Henry Morgan in 1671 is one of the most famous examples of such an attack, where the city was looted of its vast riches, much of which was never recovered.

The success of these pirates in capturing Spanish treasure added to the mystique of the Lost Bullion of the Spanish Main. The idea that some of the stolen gold and silver was buried on remote islands or hidden in secret locations fueled stories of buried treasure and pirate maps leading to untold wealth.

The Treasure Fleets: Risk, Reward, and Disaster

The Spanish treasure fleets, or *Flota de Indias*, were the lifeline of the Spanish Empire's wealth, transporting the riches of the New World back to Spain. These fleets were meticulously organized and heavily guarded, with the ships traveling in convoys to protect against pirate attacks. Despite these precautions, the fleets were often at the mercy of the elements, and many were lost to storms and shipwrecks.

The ships of the treasure fleet were loaded with bullion, gold, silver, and other valuable commodities like pearls, spices, and indigo. These riches were stored in the ship's holds, making the vessels slow and cumbersome, which only increased their vulnerability to natural disasters.

The loss of a treasure fleet was a significant blow to the Spanish Crown, both financially and symbolically. Each shipwreck represented a loss of millions of pesos, as well as the economic impact on the colonies, which relied on the fleet's protection for their trade and commerce. The loss of the 1715 Treasure Fleet, for example, was a catastrophe for Spain, as it not only represented the loss of a year's worth of New World wealth but also weakened Spain's ability to fund its wars in Europe.

The wrecks of these treasure fleets have become the focus of treasure hunters for centuries. The idea that vast sums of gold and silver lie beneath the ocean, waiting to be discovered, has lured countless adventurers to the waters of the Caribbean and the coast of Florida. Some have been successful, with portions of the 1715 Treasure Fleet being discovered by treasure hunters like Mel Fisher, who famously found the wreck of the *Nuestra Señora de Atocha* off the coast of Florida in 1985. The Atocha was part of an earlier treasure fleet lost in 1622, and its discovery yielded a haul worth hundreds of millions of dollars.

The Hunt for the Lost Bullion: Modern-Day Treasure Hunters

The legend of the Lost Bullion of the Spanish Main continues to captivate modern-day treasure hunters. Advances in technology, such as sonar and submersible vehicles, have made it possible to locate and recover shipwrecks that were previously unreachable. This has led to a new wave of treasure hunting, as adventurers and companies scour the ocean floor for the lost riches of the Spanish Empire.

One of the most famous treasure hunters of the modern era is Mel Fisher, who dedicated his life to searching for the lost Spanish galleons. Fisher's persistence paid off when he discovered the wreck of the

Atocha, a ship that had been carrying a massive cargo of gold, silver, and emeralds when it sank in a hurricane in 1622. The discovery of the *Atocha* made Fisher a legend in the world of treasure hunting and sparked renewed interest in the search for other lost Spanish treasures.

However, the hunt for the Lost Bullion of the Spanish Main is not without its challenges. Many of the shipwrecks are located in deep waters or areas with treacherous conditions, making recovery efforts difficult and dangerous. Additionally, legal battles over the ownership of recovered treasure have complicated many expeditions. Countries like Spain have claimed ownership of the treasure as part of their cultural heritage, leading to disputes with treasure hunters and salvage companies.

Despite these challenges, the allure of finding lost Spanish bullion remains strong. The possibility of discovering a treasure trove worth millions of dollars continues to draw adventurers to the Caribbean, where the promise of fortune and glory awaits those who dare to search for the lost riches of the Spanish Main.

The Cultural Impact: Legends, Myths, and Popular Culture

The story of the Lost Bullion of the Spanish Main has had a profound impact on popular culture, inspiring countless books, movies, and stories about pirates, treasure, and adventure. The romanticized image of pirates burying chests of gold on deserted islands has become a staple of pirate lore, even though there is little historical evidence to support such tales.

One of the most famous works inspired by the legend of lost Spanish treasure is Robert Louis Stevenson's *Treasure Island*, a novel that has become synonymous with the idea of buried pirate treasure. The book's depiction of treasure maps, secret islands, and ruthless pirates has shaped the popular imagination and influenced countless other works of fiction.

The legend has also found its way into film and television, with movies like the *Pirates of the Caribbean* series drawing on the imagery and mythology of the Spanish Main. The idea of lost treasure, hidden away for centuries and waiting to be found, continues to be a powerful and compelling narrative, appealing to the adventurous spirit in all of us.

The enduring popularity of the Lost Bullion of the Spanish Main is a testament to the human fascination with treasure and the unknown. It is a story that combines history, mystery, and adventure in a way that has captivated audiences for generations. Whether it is the thrill of the hunt, the allure of wealth, or the romance of the sea, the legend of the Lost Bullion of the Spanish Main remains one of the most iconic and enduring tales of treasure in history.

Conclusion: The Enduring Legacy of the Lost Bullion

The Lost Bullion of the Spanish Main is more than just a story of gold and silver lost to the depths of the ocean. It is a tale that encapsulates the ambitions, risks, and dreams of those who lived during the age of exploration and empire. The Spanish Main, with its vast wealth and perilous waters, became a stage for some of the most dramatic and legendary events in maritime history.

The legacy of the lost bullion continues to inspire treasure hunters and adventurers, drawing them to the Caribbean in search of the riches that have eluded discovery for centuries. While much of the treasure may remain lost, the stories and legends surrounding it have left an indelible mark on history and popular culture.

The Lost Bullion of the Spanish Main is a reminder of the enduring allure of treasure and the lengths to which people will go to uncover it. It is a story that will likely continue to captivate and inspire for generations to come, as the search for lost treasure is as much about the journey as it is about the destination. Whether the bullion is ever fully recovered or remains hidden beneath the waves, the legend of the Lost Bullion of the Spanish Main will endure as one of the greatest treasure tales in history.

Chapter 27: The Vanishing Crown Jewels of Nepal

The story of the Vanishing Crown Jewels of Nepal is one of the most intriguing and perplexing tales in the history of royal treasures. It is a narrative filled with political intrigue, betrayal, and mystery, centering around the unexplained disappearance of some of the most valuable and culturally significant artifacts in the history of Nepal. The jewels, once symbols of the nation's sovereignty and royal power, have become the focal point of a mystery that has puzzled historians, treasure hunters, and the Nepalese people for decades. This story is not only about the loss of material wealth but also about the impact of their disappearance on the national psyche and the enduring questions that remain unanswered.

The Historical Significance of the Nepalese Crown Jewels

The crown jewels of Nepal were more than just ornaments; they were symbols of the kingdom's heritage, sovereignty, and the divine right of the monarch to rule. These jewels, often comprising crowns, ceremonial swords, necklaces, and other regalia, were crafted with the finest materials available—gold, silver, precious stones, and intricate designs that reflected the craftsmanship of Nepalese artisans. Each piece was imbued with cultural and religious significance, often believed to carry the blessings of the gods and goddesses revered in the Hindu and Buddhist traditions.

The origins of Nepal's crown jewels can be traced back to various dynasties that ruled the region, most notably the Shah dynasty, which established the Kingdom of Nepal in the 18th century. The jewels were often passed down from one monarch to the next, each adding their own contributions to the collection, thereby increasing its value and importance over time. The jewels were not only a display of wealth and power but also a connection to the divine, with many pieces being used in religious ceremonies and rituals.

The crown itself, adorned with rubies, emeralds, diamonds, and pearls, was a masterpiece of Nepalese craftsmanship. It symbolized the unity of the kingdom, with its design incorporating elements that represented the different regions and peoples of Nepal. The ceremonial sword, another key piece of the crown jewels, was believed to have mystical powers, representing the king's duty to protect the nation and its people. Other items in the collection included necklaces and bracelets, often encrusted with gemstones and inscribed with religious texts, which were worn during significant ceremonies and festivals.

The Mysterious Disappearance: A Timeline of Events

The disappearance of the crown jewels is shrouded in mystery, with conflicting accounts and theories adding to the complexity of the case. The timeline of events leading to the jewels' vanishing is marked by political turmoil, assassinations, and shifts in power, all of which contribute to the enigma surrounding their loss.

The most widely accepted account suggests that the jewels were last seen during the reign of King Tribhuvan, who ruled Nepal from 1911 to 1955. During this period, Nepal was undergoing significant changes, with increasing pressure from political movements demanding democratic reforms and the end of the autocratic Rana rule, which had held power as hereditary prime ministers for over a century.

In 1950, King Tribhuvan fled to India in the face of growing unrest and the threat of a coup. It is believed that during this time, some of the crown jewels were smuggled out of the country, possibly as a safeguard against potential seizure by the Ranas or as a way to finance the king's exile and eventual return to power. However, this is where the trail goes cold. Upon Tribhuvan's return to Nepal in 1951, the jewels were never accounted for, leading to speculation that they had been lost, stolen, or hidden away in a secret location.

Another theory suggests that the jewels were taken by members of the royal family during the political upheavals of the 1960s and 1970s. During this period, Nepal experienced further political instability, with coups, changes in government, and the eventual establishment of a constitutional monarchy. Some historians believe that members of the royal family, fearing for their safety and the security of their wealth, may have taken the jewels and hidden them, either within Nepal or abroad. However, there is no concrete evidence to support this theory, and the whereabouts of the jewels remain unknown.

Theories and Speculation: What Happened to the Jewels?

The mystery of the Vanishing Crown Jewels of Nepal has given rise to numerous theories and speculations, each adding to the intrigue surrounding their disappearance. While no definitive answers have been found, the following are some of the most prominent theories that have been proposed:

1. **The Smuggling Theory**: As mentioned earlier, one of the most popular theories is that the jewels were smuggled out of Nepal during King Tribhuvan's exile in India. Supporters of this theory point to the chaotic political situation of the time and the need for the king to secure funds and assets to support his cause. However, the lack of documentation and the absence of any concrete evidence make this theory difficult to prove.

2. **The Hidden Treasure Theory**: Another theory posits that the jewels were hidden by the royal family or trusted aides in a secret location, possibly within Nepal. This theory is fueled by rumors of hidden royal treasures buried in remote locations, such as monasteries, palaces, or even underground vaults.

Some believe that the jewels were hidden to protect them from potential looters or political enemies, but their exact location has been lost to time.

3. **The Theft Theory**: There is also the possibility that the jewels were stolen, either by members of the royal family, government officials, or opportunistic thieves during periods of political turmoil. The lack of security and the frequent changes in power during the mid-20th century could have provided the perfect opportunity for such a theft. However, if the jewels were stolen, it is unclear why they have never surfaced on the black market or in private collections.

4. **The International Conspiracy Theory**: Some more outlandish theories suggest that the jewels were taken out of Nepal as part of an international conspiracy, possibly involving foreign governments, intelligence agencies, or even secret societies. While this theory is largely speculative and lacks credible evidence, it adds another layer of intrigue to the mystery.

5. **The Lost in Transition Theory**: Another plausible explanation is that the jewels were lost or misplaced during the numerous transitions of power and political upheavals that marked Nepal's history during the 20th century. With the frequent changes in leadership, shifts in government, and the chaos of revolution and reform, it is possible that the jewels were simply lost in the confusion and have since been forgotten or overlooked.

The Impact of the Disappearance on Nepal

The disappearance of the crown jewels had a profound impact on Nepal, both culturally and politically. The loss of such significant national symbols was a blow to the country's heritage and the monarchy's prestige. The crown jewels were not just valuable in terms of their material worth; they were also deeply connected to Nepal's history, identity, and the legitimacy of its royal family.

The mystery of the Vanishing Crown Jewels has also fueled a sense of loss and longing among the Nepalese people. For many, the jewels represent a bygone era of grandeur and sovereignty, a time when Nepal was a powerful and independent kingdom. The absence of these symbols has contributed to a sense of disconnection from that past, particularly as the country has undergone significant political changes, including the abolition of the monarchy in 2008 and the establishment of a federal democratic republic.

The loss of the crown jewels has also had a more tangible impact on Nepal's tourism and cultural heritage sectors. Had the jewels remained in Nepal, they would likely have become a major attraction for tourists and scholars, drawing visitors from around the world to see these priceless artifacts. Their disappearance has left a void in Nepal's cultural heritage, one that cannot be easily filled.

Modern Efforts to Locate the Jewels

In recent years, there have been renewed efforts to locate the missing crown jewels of Nepal. These efforts have been driven by both private individuals and government initiatives, with the hope of solving the mystery and recovering these important cultural artifacts.

One approach has been to search historical records and archives for any clues or references to the jewels' whereabouts. Researchers have combed through royal documents, government records, and even personal letters in an attempt to find any mention of the jewels or their possible hiding places. While some intriguing leads have been uncovered, none have led to a definitive discovery.

Another approach has been to investigate rumors and local legends that have persisted over the years. Stories of hidden treasure are common in Nepal, particularly in the more remote regions of the country. Some believe that the jewels may have been hidden in one of the many ancient monasteries or temples scattered throughout the Himalayas, while others suggest that they could be buried in the grounds of a royal palace or fort.

In addition to these efforts, there have also been attempts to trace the jewels through the international art and antiquities market. While it is unlikely that the crown jewels would be openly sold, there is a possibility that they could have been broken down and sold off as individual pieces. However, no credible evidence of this has been found, and the jewels remain elusive.

The Nepalese government has also expressed interest in recovering the jewels, recognizing their importance as national symbols. However, the lack of concrete evidence and the challenges of conducting such a search have made progress slow. Despite these difficulties, the search continues, driven by the hope that one day the Vanishing Crown Jewels of Nepal will be found and restored to their rightful place.

The Enduring Mystery: Why the Jewels Remain Unfound

The continued absence of the crown jewels raises many questions about why they have never been found or definitively accounted for. Several factors contribute to this enduring mystery:

1. **The Passage of Time**: The jewels disappeared over half a century ago, and with each passing year, the chances of recovering them diminish. Memories fade, records are lost, and potential witnesses pass away, making it increasingly difficult to uncover new information.

1. **Political Sensitivities**: The political nature of the jewels' disappearance has made it a sensitive topic in Nepal. The

involvement of the royal family, government officials, and the turbulent history of the mid-20th century all complicate efforts to investigate the case. There may also be a reluctance to pursue the matter too aggressively, given the potential implications for current political and social dynamics in Nepal.

2. **Lack of Evidence**: Despite various theories and rumors, there is a striking lack of concrete evidence regarding the jewels' fate. No credible sightings, transactions, or documentation have surfaced, leaving investigators with little to go on. The absence of a clear trail makes it difficult to know where to even begin looking.

3. **Possibility of Complete Destruction**: While it is an uncomfortable possibility, some have speculated that the jewels may have been destroyed, either deliberately or accidentally. If this were the case, the physical evidence of their existence would be lost forever, leaving only the mystery behind.

4. **Potential for Hidden Knowledge**: There is also the possibility that someone, somewhere, knows what happened to the jewels but has chosen to keep that information secret. Whether out of fear, loyalty, or for personal gain, this person or group may hold the key to solving the mystery but has decided not to reveal the truth.

Cultural and Symbolic Significance: The Legacy of the Vanishing Crown Jewels

The story of the Vanishing Crown Jewels of Nepal is not just a tale of lost treasure; it is a reflection of the country's complex history and the changing nature of its identity. The jewels symbolize a time when Nepal was ruled by kings who wielded both religious and political power, and their disappearance marks the end of that era.

For many Nepalese, the loss of the jewels is a poignant reminder of the challenges and upheavals their country has faced over the past century. The mystery surrounding the jewels has become a part of Nepal's cultural narrative, a story that is told and retold in the hopes of keeping the memory of the jewels alive.

The legacy of the Vanishing Crown Jewels also serves as a cautionary tale about the fragility of cultural heritage. The jewels were not just valuable objects; they were an integral part of Nepal's history and identity. Their loss underscores the importance of preserving and protecting cultural artifacts, not just for their material value but for the role they play in maintaining a connection to the past.

Conclusion: The Ongoing Quest for Answers

The mystery of the Vanishing Crown Jewels of Nepal continues to captivate the imagination of those who hear it. Despite the many theories, investigations, and efforts to uncover the truth, the jewels remain missing, their fate unknown. The story serves as a reminder of the enduring allure of lost treasure and the lengths to which people will go to uncover it.

As long as the jewels remain unfound, the mystery will endure, inspiring future generations of historians, treasure hunters, and enthusiasts to continue the search. Whether the jewels are eventually recovered or remain hidden forever, the story of the Vanishing Crown Jewels of Nepal will remain one of the most fascinating and enduring mysteries in the history of royal treasures.

Chapter 28: The High-Stakes Casino Heist

The world of casinos, with its glittering lights, rolling dice, and high-stakes gambling, has long been a magnet for those seeking fortune, fame, and sometimes infamy. Among the most audacious and cunning crimes ever attempted, the high-stakes casino heist stands out as a perfect storm of risk, reward, and relentless pursuit. It is a story that blends the thrill of gambling with the meticulous planning of a heist, where the line between luck and skill blurs, and the stakes are unimaginably high. This narrative explores the intricate details of one of the most notorious casino heists, delving into the minds of the criminals, the complexities of the operation, and the aftermath that shocked the world.

The Allure of Casinos: A World of Wealth and Opportunity

Casinos are often portrayed as the ultimate symbol of wealth and glamour, where fortunes are won and lost in the blink of an eye. For those on the right side of luck, a single night can change everything. However, for some, the allure of instant wealth leads not to the gaming tables but to the darker side of casino life—planning the perfect heist.

Casinos are filled with cash, chips, and valuables, making them prime targets for those with the audacity to attempt a robbery. The sheer volume of money that flows through a casino on a daily basis is staggering. High rollers may place bets worth millions, and the house itself often holds vast sums in vaults and safes, ready to pay out winnings or take in losses. The concentration of wealth in one location, coupled with the fast-paced and often chaotic environment, makes casinos both enticing and challenging targets for criminals.

Beyond the financial allure, casinos are also environments where risk-taking is normalized and even celebrated. This culture of risk may embolden would-be thieves, who see themselves as simply engaging in a higher-stakes version of the games being played on the casino floor. The thrill of the heist, the idea of beating the house at its own game, and the potential for a massive payout are powerful motivators for those willing to risk everything in pursuit of a casino's riches.

Planning the Heist: A Complex Web of Deception

Executing a successful casino heist requires more than just nerve—it demands meticulous planning, a deep understanding of the casino's operations, and often, inside knowledge. The complexity of such an operation cannot be overstated; it involves not only outwitting the casino's sophisticated security systems but also coordinating a team of individuals, each with a specific role to play.

The first step in planning a high-stakes casino heist is gathering intelligence. This often involves spending time in the casino, observing the layout, understanding the flow of money, and identifying potential vulnerabilities. Casinos are designed to be secure, with multiple layers of protection, including surveillance cameras, security personnel, and advanced alarm systems. To overcome these obstacles, the heist's masterminds must be highly skilled and creative.

In some cases, the planning phase may also involve recruiting insiders—employees who work within the casino and have access to critical information. These insiders can provide valuable details about security protocols, shift changes, and the locations of vaults or high-value assets. They may also be able to manipulate systems from within, disabling alarms, providing access to restricted areas, or even directly participating in the theft.

Timing is another crucial element of the heist. The criminals must choose the right moment to strike, often during peak hours when the casino is crowded and distractions are plentiful, or alternatively, during quieter times when fewer security personnel are on duty. The timing must also account for the movement of money within the casino, ensuring that the heist occurs when the maximum amount of cash or chips is available.

The team assembled for the heist must be carefully selected, with each member bringing a specific skill set to the operation. This could include experts in safecracking, surveillance, electronics, or even psychology, capable of manipulating people or situations to the team's advantage. The roles must be clearly defined, and everyone must work in perfect coordination to ensure the success of the operation.

Finally, the escape plan is as critical as the heist itself. Casinos are often located in busy urban areas, with law enforcement able to respond quickly. The criminals must have a well-thought-out plan for evading capture, whether it involves disguises, multiple getaway vehicles, or even the use of underground tunnels or other unconventional routes. In some cases, the escape plan may also include measures to divert attention, such as setting off alarms or creating other distractions.

The Execution: Tension and High Stakes

When the time comes to execute the heist, every detail must go according to plan. The criminals must remain calm under pressure, knowing that any mistake could result in immediate capture or worse. The tension is palpable as the operation unfolds, with each member of the team playing their part to perfection.

In one of the most famous high-stakes casino heists, the criminals used a combination of deception, brute force, and advanced technology to achieve their goal. The heist began with a diversion—a false alarm triggered in a different part of the casino, drawing security personnel away from the vault. Meanwhile, the team gained access to the vault through a combination of insider assistance and sophisticated hacking, bypassing the casino's security systems.

Once inside the vault, the criminals worked quickly, knowing that time was of the essence. They used high-powered drills and explosives to break into the safes, taking care to avoid triggering any secondary alarms. As they filled their bags with cash, chips, and valuables, the tension mounted. Every second counted, and the team knew that any delay could mean the difference between success and failure.

The final stage of the heist was the escape. The criminals had planned their getaway with precision, using multiple vehicles to confuse pursuers and switching disguises to avoid detection. In some cases, they even used decoys—vehicles or individuals meant to draw attention away from the real escape route. The adrenaline was high as they made their way out of the casino and into the night, knowing that the most dangerous part of the operation was behind them.

The Aftermath: Investigation and Pursuit

The aftermath of a high-stakes casino heist is often as dramatic as the heist itself. Once the crime is discovered, the casino immediately goes into lockdown, with law enforcement called to the scene. The investigation begins almost immediately, with detectives and forensic experts working to piece together what happened.

Casinos have extensive surveillance systems, and the footage from the night of the heist is scrutinized in minute detail. Every angle is reviewed, every shadow analyzed, as investigators search for clues that could lead to the identification of the criminals. They also examine the scene for physical evidence—fingerprints, DNA, or any other trace left behind by the perpetrators.

In many cases, the investigation quickly expands beyond the casino, with law enforcement agencies collaborating across jurisdictions to track down the criminals. The stolen money or chips are often marked, making them difficult to use without being detected. As a result, the criminals may attempt to launder the money or convert the chips into cash through intermediaries, further complicating the investigation.

The pressure on the criminals increases as the investigation progresses. They must stay one step ahead of the law, constantly moving, changing identities, and avoiding any behavior that might draw attention. The psychological toll of living on the run can be immense, with the constant fear of capture hanging over them.

In some cases, the criminals are eventually caught, either through a slip-up or as a result of a relentless pursuit by law enforcement. The penalties for such crimes are severe, often involving lengthy prison sentences and significant financial restitution. However, in other cases, the criminals may evade capture, their identities remaining a mystery as they disappear into the shadows.

Famous Casino Heists: Case Studies of Daring and Deception

The history of casino heists is filled with infamous cases, each with its own unique set of circumstances and outcomes. Some of these heists have become legendary, inspiring books, movies, and television shows. Below are a few examples of some of the most notable casino heists in history:

1. **The Stardust Heist (1992):** One of the largest casino heists in history, the Stardust Heist involved a single man, Bill Brennan, who worked as a cashier at the Stardust Casino in Las Vegas. Over time, Brennan carefully planned his heist, taking advantage of his position of trust within the casino. On September 22, 1992, he calmly walked out of the casino with

a bag containing over $500,000 in cash and chips. Brennan disappeared without a trace and remains one of the most successful casino robbers in history. Despite extensive investigations, he was never caught, and his whereabouts remain unknown.

2. **The Bellagio Heist (2010)**: The Bellagio Heist is another famous example of a high-stakes casino robbery. On December 14, 2010, a man named Anthony Carleo, wearing a full-face motorcycle helmet, walked into the Bellagio Casino in Las Vegas and approached a craps table. Armed with a gun, Carleo demanded chips from the dealer, making off with approximately $1.5 million worth of high-denomination chips. However, Carleo's downfall came when he attempted to sell the stolen chips, which were marked and easily traceable. He was eventually apprehended by the police and sentenced to prison.

3. **The Ritz Casino Heist (2004)**: The Ritz Casino in London was the target of a sophisticated heist in March 2004. The criminals, using a laser scanner and a computer, managed to predict the outcome of the roulette wheel with remarkable accuracy. By placing bets at the last possible moment, they were able to win approximately £1.3 million. The heist was so technologically advanced that it took the casino some time to realize they had been cheated. Although the criminals were arrested, they were never convicted, as their method was deemed not to be technically illegal.

Cultural Impact and Legacy: The Fascination with Casino Heists

The high-stakes casino heist has captured the public's imagination like few other crimes. The combination of glamour, danger, and the allure of easy money makes these stories endlessly fascinating. The image of suave, sophisticated criminals outwitting the house and walking away with millions is a powerful one, and it has been immortalized in countless books, films, and television series.

Movies like "Ocean's Eleven" and its sequels have romanticized the idea of the casino heist, portraying it as a high-stakes game of wits between the criminals and the casino. These films have contributed to the cultural mythology of the casino heist, depicting the criminals as likable rogues who use their intelligence and charm to pull off the impossible.

The real-life cases, however, are often far less glamorous. The reality of a casino heist is one of meticulous planning, high risks, and often severe consequences. The criminals involved are not always the charming masterminds portrayed in fiction, and the aftermath of the heist can be grim, with long prison sentences, financial ruin, and lives destroyed.

Despite this, the allure of the casino heist endures. It speaks to a deep-seated fascination with the idea of outsmarting the system, of beating the odds in a game where the house always seems to win. The stories of these heists continue to be told and retold, each one adding to the rich tapestry of legends that surround the world of casinos.

Conclusion: The Enduring Mystery of the High-Stakes Casino Heist

The high-stakes casino heist is a crime that occupies a unique place in the annals of criminal history. It is a crime that combines the thrill of gambling with the meticulous planning of a heist, where the line between luck and skill blurs, and the stakes are unimaginably high. The stories of these heists, whether successful or not, continue to captivate and intrigue, offering a glimpse into a world where the rewards are great, but the risks are even greater.

As long as casinos exist, and as long as the human desire for wealth and excitement endures, the high-stakes casino heist will remain a part of our cultural imagination. Whether through real-life events or fictional tales, the legend of the casino heist will continue to be told, reminding us of the enduring allure of risk, reward, and the ultimate gamble.

216

Chapter 29: The Great Train Robbery: Modern Edition

The notion of a train robbery might evoke images of the Wild West, where masked outlaws on horseback pursued steam-powered locomotives, guns blazing as they made off with bags of cash and valuable cargo. However, the concept of a train robbery is far from being a relic of the past. In the modern era, the Great Train Robbery has taken on new dimensions, blending traditional criminal tactics with advanced technology, sophisticated planning, and high-stakes outcomes. The modern edition of this crime is a testament to how the fundamental appeal of hijacking valuable goods in transit continues to evolve, adapting to contemporary challenges and opportunities. This detailed exploration will delve into the motivations, methods, and consequences of modern train robberies, shedding light on a crime that, while less common than in the past, remains a potent symbol of daring and defiance against authority.

The Evolution of Train Robbery: From Outlaws to High-Tech Criminals

Train robbery as a concept has undergone a significant transformation over the years. In the 19th and early 20th centuries, these heists were often carried out by gangs of outlaws who used brute force and the element of surprise to overpower train crews and passengers. The robberies were typically executed in remote areas where the robbers could escape into the wilderness, far from the reach of law enforcement. The loot from these robberies often consisted of cash, gold, and other valuables being transported between cities.

As time progressed, the advent of modern security measures and changes in the way goods and money were transported led to a decline in traditional train robberies. However, the allure of robbing a train—a moving treasure trove of valuable goods—never entirely disappeared. Instead, the methods used to carry out these heists evolved, reflecting changes in technology, transportation, and criminal enterprise.

In the modern era, train robberies are far less common than they once were, but when they do occur, they are often far more sophisticated and complex than their historical counterparts. Today's train robbers are likely to be highly organized, utilizing advanced technology and careful planning to execute their crimes. These modern heists often involve not only the physical theft of goods but also cyber elements, where criminals hack into logistics systems, disable security measures, and manipulate digital records to cover their tracks.

The Anatomy of a Modern Train Heist: Planning and Execution

Executing a modern train robbery requires meticulous planning and coordination. Unlike the train robberies of old, which relied heavily on brute force and opportunism, modern train heists are carefully orchestrated operations that involve a deep understanding of the logistics, security measures, and technology used in rail transport.

- **Intelligence Gathering and Target Selection**

The first step in planning a modern train robbery is selecting the target. This often involves extensive research and intelligence gathering. The criminals must identify a train carrying high-value goods, such as electronics, luxury items, or precious metals. These trains are often part of complex supply chains, moving goods between manufacturing facilities, distribution centers, and retail outlets.

To identify a suitable target, the criminals may infiltrate the companies involved in the supply chain, gaining inside information about shipment schedules, cargo contents, and security measures. Alternatively, they may use cyber tactics to hack into logistics systems, gaining access to the same information. The goal is to pinpoint a train that carries a significant amount of valuable cargo but is vulnerable to attack.

- **Analyzing Security Measures**

Modern trains are equipped with a variety of security measures designed to protect their cargo. These can include onboard security personnel, surveillance cameras, GPS tracking systems, and secure containers. In some cases, the cargo may be insured and monitored by private security firms, adding an additional layer of protection.

To overcome these challenges, the criminals must thoroughly analyze the security measures in place and identify potential weaknesses. This could involve hacking into the train's systems to disable security cameras, jam GPS signals, or manipulate electronic locks on cargo containers. Alternatively, they may use social engineering tactics to deceive or manipulate security personnel into providing access to the train or its cargo.

- **Coordinating the Heist**

Once the target has been selected and the security measures analyzed, the criminals must coordinate the heist itself. This often involves assembling a team of specialists, each with a specific role to play. For example, one team member might be responsible for disabling the train's security systems, while another handles the physical theft of the cargo. The team may also include drivers and lookouts who help ensure a swift and safe getaway.

Timing is critical in executing a modern train robbery. The criminals must strike at the right moment, often while the train is in transit through a remote area where law enforcement response times are slower. In some cases, the criminals may even manipulate the train's schedule or route, creating a situation where the train is more vulnerable to attack.

- **The Getaway and Aftermath**

The getaway is one of the most challenging aspects of a modern train robbery. The criminals must quickly transfer the stolen goods from the train to waiting vehicles, often under the cover of darkness or in a remote location. Speed and efficiency are critical, as any delay increases the risk of detection by law enforcement or security personnel.

Once the stolen goods are secured, the criminals must then find a way to move or sell them without attracting attention. This often involves working with fences or black-market dealers who specialize in converting stolen goods into cash. The criminals may also use false documentation or smuggling networks to move the goods across borders, further complicating efforts to recover the stolen items.

The aftermath of a modern train robbery can be complex, with law enforcement agencies conducting extensive investigations to identify and apprehend the criminals involved. These investigations often involve collaboration between multiple agencies, including local police, national law enforcement, and international organizations such as Interpol. The use of advanced forensic techniques, surveillance footage, and digital evidence is critical in tracking down the perpetrators and recovering the stolen goods.

Notable Cases of Modern Train Robberies

While modern train robberies are relatively rare, there have been several high-profile cases in recent years that highlight the continued appeal and challenges of this type of crime.

- **The Antwerp Diamond Heist (2003)**

One of the most infamous modern train robberies is the Antwerp Diamond Heist, which took place in Belgium in 2003. While not technically a train robbery in the traditional sense, the heist involved the theft of diamonds and other precious stones from a train transporting them to the Antwerp Diamond Center. The criminals, led by Leonardo Notarbartolo, used a combination of high-tech gadgets and old-fashioned criminal know-how to bypass the train's security systems and make off with an estimated $100 million in gems.

The Antwerp Diamond Heist is a prime example of how modern train robberies can involve a mix of physical and cyber tactics. The criminals used sophisticated hacking techniques to disable the train's alarm systems and access the cargo. They also employed traditional methods, such as safecracking and cutting through metal barriers, to gain entry to the train's secure containers.

- **The Great Cargo Theft (2013)**

In 2013, a group of criminals executed a daring train robbery in Spain, targeting a train carrying electronic goods worth millions of euros. The criminals used a combination of brute force and precision to hijack the train while it was in transit, overpowering the crew and transferring the cargo to waiting trucks. The heist was carried out with military-like precision, with the criminals escaping before law enforcement could respond.

The Great Cargo Theft is an example of how modern train robberies can still involve physical violence and the use of force. The criminals in this case were well-organized and prepared, using weapons and intimidation to ensure the success of the heist. The aftermath of the robbery involved a massive manhunt, with law enforcement agencies across Europe working together to track down the perpetrators.

- **The Paris-Luxury Goods Heist (2015)**

In 2015, a train carrying luxury goods from Paris to Milan was the target of a sophisticated robbery. The criminals, believed to be part of an international organized crime ring, used drones to monitor the train's movements and security measures. They then used specialized equipment to breach the train's cargo containers and make off with millions of euros worth of designer clothing, handbags, and accessories.

The Paris-Luxury Goods Heist is a striking example of how modern technology is being used to execute train robberies. The use of drones allowed the criminals to conduct surveillance on the train from a safe distance, while the specialized equipment enabled them to bypass the train's security systems with ease. The heist also highlighted the global nature of modern train robberies, with the stolen goods being quickly moved across borders and sold on the black market.

Challenges and Risks: The High Stakes of Modern Train Robbery

Modern train robberies are fraught with challenges and risks, making them a dangerous and difficult crime to pull off. The potential rewards are significant, but the risks of capture, injury, or even death are equally high. The following are some of the key challenges and risks faced by those who attempt a modern train robbery:

- **Advanced Security Measures**

Modern trains are equipped with state-of-the-art security measures designed to prevent theft and protect valuable cargo. These can include GPS tracking, surveillance cameras, secure containers, and alarm systems. Overcoming these security measures requires a high level of technical expertise and access to specialized equipment, making it difficult for all but the most skilled criminals to succeed.

- **Law Enforcement Response**

Law enforcement agencies are well aware of the potential for train robberies and are prepared to respond quickly and decisively when they occur. Modern police forces have access to advanced forensic techniques, digital evidence, and collaboration with international organizations, making it difficult for criminals to evade capture. The risks of being caught are high, and those who are apprehended can face lengthy prison sentences and substantial fines.

- **Complex Logistics**

Executing a modern train robbery involves complex logistics, including timing the heist

correctly, coordinating the movements of multiple vehicles, and transferring the stolen goods quickly and efficiently. Any mistake in the planning or execution of the heist can result in failure, with the criminals being caught before they can make their escape.

- **Legal Consequences**

The legal consequences of a modern train robbery can be severe. Those who are caught and convicted can face lengthy prison sentences, substantial fines, and the forfeiture of any assets gained from the crime. In addition, the stolen goods are often recovered and returned to their rightful owners, leaving the criminals with nothing to show for their efforts.

- **Public Perception**

Modern train robberies, while rare, often attract significant media attention, leading to increased public awareness and scrutiny. The romanticized image of the train robber as a daring outlaw is often overshadowed by the harsh realities of the crime, including the potential for violence, injury, and death. The public perception of train robberies as a dangerous and reckless crime can also lead to increased pressure on law enforcement to apprehend and prosecute those involved.

The Legacy of Modern Train Robberies: A Crime That Endures

The modern edition of the Great Train Robbery is a testament to the enduring appeal of this type of crime. Despite the challenges and risks involved, the allure of hijacking a train and making off with valuable cargo continues to captivate the imagination of criminals and the public alike. While the methods and technology used in modern train robberies have evolved, the fundamental elements of the crime—planning, execution, and the thrill of the heist—remain the same.

As long as valuable goods are transported by rail, the potential for train robberies will continue to exist. The crime may become more rare and difficult to execute, but it is unlikely to disappear entirely. The legacy of the Great Train Robbery, in all its forms, will endure, reminding us of the enduring appeal of risk, reward, and the ultimate gamble.

Chapter 30: The Shanghai Bank Heist

The Shanghai Bank Heist is a legendary event that epitomizes the audacity, precision, and high stakes associated with large-scale criminal operations in one of the world's most vibrant and economically pivotal cities. As a financial hub with a rich history of international trade and investment, Shanghai has long been a focal point for wealth and opportunity. This also makes it a prime target for those daring enough to attempt a heist in its heavily guarded financial institutions. The Shanghai Bank Heist, in particular, stands out not only for its sheer scale but also for the complex planning, international intrigue, and the dramatic aftermath that followed. This detailed exploration will delve into the intricacies of this heist, examining the motivations, the meticulous planning, the execution, and the far-reaching consequences that make it one of the most infamous bank robberies in modern history.

Historical Context: Shanghai's Financial Powerhouse Status

To understand the significance of the Shanghai Bank Heist, it is essential to first appreciate the city's status as a financial powerhouse. Shanghai, often referred to as the "Paris of the East," has a long history of economic prosperity, dating back to its days as a major port city in the 19th and early 20th centuries. With the advent of modern banking and finance, Shanghai quickly became home to numerous financial institutions, including both domestic and international banks. These banks, housed in grand buildings along the iconic Bund, held vast reserves of cash, gold, and other valuable assets, making them prime targets for criminal enterprises.

By the early 21st century, Shanghai had solidified its position as a global financial center, with its banks playing a crucial role in the international economy. The city's financial institutions were known for their advanced security measures, making them seemingly impregnable fortresses in the world of high finance. However, the allure of the vast wealth contained within these banks proved irresistible to a group of highly skilled criminals who were determined to pull off the heist of a lifetime.

Motivation Behind the Heist: The Lure of Enormous Wealth

The motivations driving the perpetrators of the Shanghai Bank Heist were multifaceted, but at their core was the pursuit of enormous wealth. The target bank, located in the heart of Shanghai's financial district, was one of the most secure and well-guarded institutions in the city. It was known to house large amounts of cash, gold bullion, and other valuable assets, both in its vaults and in transit between the bank and other financial centers.

For the criminals involved, the potential rewards of the heist were astronomical. Successfully robbing the bank would not only yield a significant financial windfall but also confer a level of infamy and notoriety that would cement their place in the annals of criminal history. The heist was not merely about money; it was about achieving the near-impossible, outsmarting the system, and pulling off a feat that would be remembered for decades to come.

Planning the Heist: A Masterclass in Criminal Strategy

The Shanghai Bank Heist was a masterclass in criminal strategy, involving meticulous planning and coordination over an extended period. The criminals knew that they would be facing one of the most secure banks in the world, with state-of-the-art security systems, armed guards, and round-the-clock surveillance. To succeed, they would need to overcome these formidable defenses with precision and efficiency.

- **Gathering Intelligence**

The first phase of the heist involved gathering detailed intelligence on the bank's operations, security measures, and personnel. This was no small task, as the bank's security protocols were designed to be nearly impenetrable. The criminals employed a variety of methods to collect the necessary information, including infiltrating the bank's staff, hacking into computer systems, and conducting surveillance on the bank's physical premises.

The intelligence-gathering phase was critical to the success of the heist, as it provided the criminals with valuable insights into the bank's vulnerabilities. They learned the layout of the bank, the timing of security patrols, the locations of surveillance cameras, and the schedules of cash and asset transfers. This information allowed them to identify the best time and method for carrying out the heist.

- **Assembling the Team**

With the intelligence in hand, the next step was assembling a team of specialists who could execute the heist. The criminals knew that they would need a diverse set of skills to pull off such a complex operation, so they recruited individuals with expertise in various areas, including hacking, safecracking, logistics, and security.

Each member of the team was carefully selected for their specific abilities and their ability to work under pressure. The team also included individuals with connections to the black market, who could help launder the stolen assets and move them out of the country. The criminals understood that the success of the heist depended on the seamless coordination of these specialists, so they spent considerable time planning and rehearsing every aspect of the operation.

- **Timing and Logistics**

Timing was crucial to the success of the Shanghai Bank Heist. The criminals needed to strike at the perfect moment, when the bank's security measures were at their weakest. They also needed to ensure that their getaway was swift and undetected, as any delay could result in their capture.

The logistics of the heist were meticulously planned, with every detail accounted for. The criminals arranged for a fleet of vehicles to transport the stolen assets, and they mapped out multiple escape routes to avoid detection. They also secured safe houses where they could lay low after the heist, and they established communication channels that would allow them to stay in contact without being traced.

Execution of the Heist: The Night of the Robbery

The night of the robbery was the culmination of months of planning and preparation. The criminals knew that they had only one chance to get it right, so they executed the heist with military-like precision.

- **Infiltration and Neutralization of Security**

The first phase of the heist involved infiltrating the bank and neutralizing its security systems. The criminals used their insider knowledge to bypass the bank's external defenses, including surveillance cameras and motion detectors. Once inside, they used a combination of hacking and physical manipulation to disable the bank's alarm systems and unlock the vault.

The criminals also took steps to neutralize the bank's security personnel. They used non-lethal methods, such as tranquilizers and gas, to incapacitate the guards without alerting the authorities. This allowed them to move freely within the bank and access the vault without interference.

- **Accessing the Vault**

The most challenging part of the heist was accessing the vault, which was protected by multiple layers of security. The criminals had prepared for this by bringing specialized equipment, including high-powered drills, explosives, and electronic devices designed to bypass the vault's locking mechanisms.

The process of breaking into the vault was slow and painstaking, as the criminals had to work carefully to avoid triggering any alarms. They used a combination of brute force and technical expertise to breach the vault's defenses, eventually gaining access to its contents.

- **The Getaway**

With the vault breached and the stolen assets in hand, the criminals faced the final challenge: escaping undetected. They executed their getaway plan with precision, loading the stolen assets into waiting vehicles and dispersing through multiple escape routes. The criminals had planned for every contingency, including the possibility of a police chase, and they were able to evade capture by using decoy vehicles and safe houses.

Aftermath and Investigation: The Global Hunt for the Perpetrators

The aftermath of the Shanghai Bank Heist was a frenzy of activity, as law enforcement agencies launched a massive investigation to track down the perpetrators and recover the stolen assets. The heist had been executed with such precision that the authorities were initially left with few leads, but they were determined to bring the criminals to justice.

- **The Investigation**

The investigation into the Shanghai Bank Heist was one of the largest and most complex in the city's history. The authorities used a combination of forensic analysis, surveillance footage, and digital forensics to piece together the events of the night. They also conducted extensive interviews with bank employees, security personnel, and anyone who might have had information about the heist.

The investigation quickly expanded beyond Shanghai, as the authorities realized that the criminals had likely fled the country. Interpol and other international law enforcement agencies were brought in to assist with the investigation, and a global manhunt was launched to track down the perpetrators.

- **The Role of Technology**

Technology played a crucial role in both the execution of the heist and the subsequent investigation. The criminals had used advanced hacking techniques to disable the bank's security systems, and they had employed sophisticated communication methods to coordinate their activities. The authorities, in turn, used technology to track down the criminals, analyzing digital footprints, tracing financial transactions, and monitoring communications.

The use of technology in the Shanghai Bank Heist highlighted the growing importance of cybercrime in modern criminal enterprises. It also underscored the challenges that law enforcement agencies face in combating such crimes, as the criminals are often able to stay one step ahead of the authorities by using cutting-edge technology.

- **The Global Manhunt**

The global manhunt for the perpetrators of the Shanghai Bank Heist was a dramatic and high-stakes operation. The criminals had gone to great lengths to cover their tracks, using false identities, encrypted communications, and offshore accounts to avoid detection. However, the authorities were relentless in their pursuit, using every tool at their disposal to track down the criminals and recover the stolen assets.

The manhunt eventually led to several arrests, though not all of the criminals were apprehended. Some managed to evade capture, disappearing into the criminal underworld with their share of the loot. The stolen assets were also only partially recovered, with much of the money and gold believed to have been laundered and sold on the black market.

The Impact of the Heist: A Cautionary Tale

The Shanghai Bank Heist had far-reaching consequences, both for the criminals involved and for the banking industry as a whole. It served as a stark reminder of the vulnerabilities that exist even in the most secure institutions, and it prompted a reevaluation of security protocols in banks around the world.

- **Changes in Bank Security**

In the wake of the heist, banks in Shanghai and other major financial centers implemented a series of security upgrades to prevent similar incidents from occurring. These upgrades included the adoption of more advanced surveillance systems, the use of biometric authentication, and the installation of reinforced vaults and safes.

Banks also began to place a greater emphasis on cybersecurity, recognizing the growing threat posed by hackers and other cybercriminals. This shift in focus led to the development of more sophisticated digital defenses, including encryption, intrusion detection systems, and real-time monitoring of financial transactions.

- **Legal and Regulatory Reforms**

The Shanghai Bank Heist also prompted a wave of legal and regulatory reforms aimed at strengthening the banking industry's resilience to criminal activity. Governments around the world introduced new laws and regulations designed to combat money laundering, improve transparency, and enhance cooperation between law enforcement agencies.

These reforms had a significant impact on the global banking industry, leading to increased scrutiny of financial transactions and greater accountability for financial institutions. However, they also placed new burdens on banks, requiring them to invest in additional security measures and comply with a growing array of regulations.

- **The Legacy of the Heist**

The legacy of the Shanghai Bank Heist is one of both caution and fascination. While the heist itself was a criminal act, it captured the public's imagination and became the subject of numerous books, documentaries, and films. The audacity of the criminals, the complexity of their plan, and the high-stakes nature of the heist made it a story that resonated with people around the world.

At the same time, the heist served as a cautionary tale for the banking industry, highlighting the need for constant vigilance and adaptation in the face of evolving threats. It underscored the importance of security in an increasingly interconnected and digitized world, and it reminded banks of the ever-present risk of criminal activity.

Conclusion: The Enduring Mystery

The Shanghai Bank Heist remains one of the most infamous and intriguing bank robberies in history. It is a story of meticulous planning, daring execution, and the relentless pursuit of justice. While much of the heist remains shrouded in mystery, its impact on the banking industry and its place in the annals of criminal history are undeniable. The heist serves as a reminder of the lengths to which criminals will go to achieve their goals, and the importance of remaining ever-vigilant in the face of such threats.

Epilogue

As we close this journey through some of history's most audacious and infamous heists, one thing becomes abundantly clear: the allure of the perfect crime remains timeless. From the back alleys of bustling cities to the high seas and the vast digital expanse of cyberspace, each heist we've explored is a testament to human ingenuity, ambition, and often, sheer desperation.

While these stories vary in setting, scale, and outcome, they all share a common theme: the delicate dance between order and chaos, law and lawlessness. The criminals behind these heists were not just thieves but also tacticians, risk-takers, and in many cases, unwitting revolutionaries who exposed the vulnerabilities of the systems they exploited. They showed us that even the most secure vaults could be breached, the most protected art stolen, and the most encrypted data hacked.

For some of these criminals, the heist was a means to an end—an escape from poverty, a stand against perceived injustice, or simply a quest for thrill and notoriety. For others, it was an art form, a pursuit driven by meticulous planning, sharp intellect, and an understanding of human psychology. Whatever their motivations, these individuals became part of a larger story—a story about human nature, ambition, and the eternal conflict between good and evil.

Yet, what these stories also remind us is that crime, no matter how well-executed, rarely pays in the end. The pursuit of wealth, fame, or revenge through illicit means often comes at a high cost. Many of those who carried out these heists eventually faced justice, lived in fear, or suffered personal losses that outweighed their gains. Some remain nameless ghosts, their identities lost to history, their stories lingering as unanswered questions.

But perhaps the most intriguing aspect of these heists is their ability to capture the imagination. They fascinate us, not merely because of their daring or their success but because they speak to something deeper within us—a desire to challenge the status quo, to dream beyond our limits, and, perhaps, to find out what we're truly capable of under pressure. They remind us of the thin line between right and wrong, the complexity of human motivation, and the unpredictable nature of fate.

As we end this collection of tales, remember that behind every heist is a story of risk and reward, of ambition and consequence. They are a mirror reflecting society's flaws and its strengths, its vices and its virtues. In the end, the stories of these infamous heists are not just about crime—they're about the enduring human spirit that drives us to push boundaries, for better or for worse.

And so, we leave these stories with a final thought: in a world where the line between order and chaos is ever-shifting, the true test of character lies not in the heist but in the choices we make every day. For it is our decisions, more than any vault, lock, or code, that define who we are and what we become.

Until the next heist, keep your eyes open and your imaginations alive. After all, the greatest stories are yet to be written.

The End.